THE
ART of
ASKING

A Handbook for Successful Fund Raising

Paul H. Schneiter

Walker and Company · New York

For Pat

First published in the United States of America in 1978 by the Walker Publishing
Company, Inc.
Published simultaneously in Canada by Beaverbooks, Limited, Pickering,
Ontario
ISBN: 0-8027-0587-1
Library of Congress Catalog Card Number: 77-78993
Printed in the United States of America

10 9 8 7 6 5 4 3 2 1

Contents

Preface

Fund-raising is an intriguing art. It demands mastery of an odd assortment of skills, some of which seem altogether incompatible. The successful fund-raiser must be both gentle and aggressive, modest and proud, quiet and outspoken. In recent years fund-raising has been further complicated by dramatic changes in both technology and taxation.

Nevertheless, American fund-raising is thriving as never before. Fund-raisers, amateur and professional, are at the very center of some of the most significant events in American community and national life. They are also at the center of an enormous financial enterprise. If you count contributions of money and of labor in the form of volunteer work, the dollar value of American philanthropy exceeds $50 billion a year, according to the Commission on Private Philanthropy and Public Needs. The amount Americans give has increased every year since 1910. Outlook for the decade ahead? More of the same.

Millions of Americans are directly involved in fund-raising management and solicitation. Relatively few of these, however, are seasoned veterans. Some are simply doing their civic duty, such as the auto dealer who agrees to head up the United Way campaign in his town. Some are former athletes and coaches, insurance agents, and real estate men hired by junior colleges or relatively small hospitals. Some are teachers who have taken on an additional assignment. Some are active members of their faith who have heeded the call of their religious leaders. Some are housewives doing their part for PTA and Little League. And some are very young, such as the Girl Scouts who sell cookies door to door.

Many, frankly, are scared. And they have a right to be: In almost no other endeavor is one's performance so visible and measurable. Most are woefully unprepared for their fund-raising roles. Selling automobiles or insurance is one thing, but asking people to give their money to a cause, institution or program is quite another.

And make no mistake: Asking *is* the heart of the matter. You *must* ask if you hope to receive. Furthermore, many people not only expect you to ask, they actually look forward to it. According to Dr. Ernest Dichter, nationally recognized motivational psychologist, being asked helps to satisfy the human need to be wanted, to be courted, to play God.

How do people learn the art of asking? Do they study it in college? No—it isn't taught there. Do they learn it from friends or business associates? Not really. Do they learn it in three-day seminars in Las Vegas? They try. Do they learn it by trial and error? Probably. And the results are usually disappointing, if not disastrous. At best they waste too much time, talent and material. At worst, they tarnish otherwise respectable careers as well as the name of the cause for which they seek funds.

The purpose of this book is to help people learn the art of asking. It is a comprehensive, practical, no-nonsense guide to fund-raising (it does not, however, cover governmental grant-making). It is short on theory and long on practice. It is suitable for both individual and institutional use. Although it was written expressly for those in the range of zero to moderate fund-raising experience, veteran fund-raisers will find that it offers provocative new perspectives and insights.

This book is based on my many years of experience with a large, diversified organization that has successfully raised millions of dollars for many different kinds of institutions. Included among these are the largest church-owned university and junior college in America. Although my experience has touched all aspects of fund-raising, my specialty has been fund-raising communication. That circumstance accounts for the title of the book as well as for its special emphasis on the tools and techniques of asking.

My hope is that the book will help those whose causes are just.

ACKNOWLEDGMENTS

The author gratefully acknowledges the assistance of his colleagues and friends in The Development Office of The Church of Jesus Christ of Latter-day Saints whose knowledge, experience and willingness to help made this book possible. Special thanks are expressed to Donald T. Nelson, Carl W. Bacon, John J. Cunningham, Ronald G. Hyde, Sharon Maxey, James K. Olson, Kenneth W. Porter, Barry P. Preator, Kimber O. Ricks, Kenneth "J" Taylor, and Richard L. Whittaker.

In addition, the author wishes to recognize the thoughtful and valuable contributions of the following individuals and organizations: Allen C. Best; James S. Gardner; Robert M. Holcombe; Arthur J. Horton; Mark J. Howard; Neal H. Hurwitz; Michael M. Kawasaki; Anne Klepper; Kerry P. McClanahan; Helen L. O'Rourke; Dwight V. Roberts; Alan R. Robinson; Fred Schnaue; Howard M. Schwartz; Con Squires; Alfred G. Wardley; Byron Welch; Stephen Wertheimer and Richard K. Winslow. Also, Abingdon Press; American Association of Fund-Raising Counsel, Inc.; American Cancer Society, Inc.; Boys' Club of Utah County; Brakeley, John Price Jones Inc.; Brigham Young University; The Conference

Board; Council for Financial Aid to Education, Inc.; Council for the Advancement and Support of Education; Council on Foundations; CS Writing and Design Services; Elmcrest Children's Center, Inc.; Howard M. Schwartz & Associates, Inc.; Lehigh University; National Information Bureau, Inc.; Oram International Corporation; Park-Tudor School; Philanthropic Advisory Service (a division of the Council of Better Business Bureaus, Inc.); Princeton University; Ricks College; United Way of America; University of Colorado Foundation; Weber State College; and Welch Associates, Inc.

The following figures are reproduced by permission of The Development Office, The Church of Jesus Christ of Latter-day Saints, Provo, Utah: 4-4, 4-5, 4-11, 4-12, 4-14, 4-16, 4-18, 4-20, 6-1, 6-2, 6-3, 6-4, 6-7, 6-8. Figure 4-10 is reproduced by permission of Weber State College, Ogden, Utah. Figure 4-21 is reproduced by permission of Utah Valley Hospital, Provo, Utah. Figure 5-1 is reproduced by permission of Boys' Club of Utah County.

Chapter One

WHO GIVES —
AND TO WHOM?

Americans are the most generous people on earth, and American philanthropy is the envy of the world.

Sound familiar? Chances are it does—or at least some variation of it. And unlike some cherished American ideas that have fallen on hard times, this one, it's good to know, has not: Americans *are* the most generous people on earth, and American philanthropy *is* the envy of the world.

Proof? From 1910 through 1976, Americans contributed more than *$412 billion* to charitable causes. And on every day of 1976 alone, Americans gave away an average of $80,547,945! In addition, 37 million of us—24 percent of the entire adult population—devoted time to volunteer work in 1976. No other people anywhere on this planet are even remotely as charitable.

In short, while philanthropy has Greek roots (literally "lov-

NOTE: Many of the fund-raising figures and facts reported herein are from annual reports published by the American Association of Fund-Raising Counsel, Inc. The author acknowledges with grateful appreciation the valuable assistance of this organization.

ing mankind"), it has flourished and flowered in *American* soil. Americans are its pre-eminent practitioners, both as givers and receivers.

This chapter sets the American philanthropic scene for you. The purpose here is to help you to understand the unique drama of which you are a part, and to prepare yourself for your important role in it. Specifically, the information herein will help you to evaluate the giving patterns of individuals, foundations and corporations (the three sources of United States philanthropic support), and to relate them to your cause. The amounts these sources contribute, their principal interests and some trends for the future are also identified. Finally, the major ways in which individuals give, from simple cash gifts to life-income agreements, are introduced.

To give you the proper perspective for the information that follows, here is an overview of American philanthropy—a quick look at who gave and who received from 1967 through 1976:

Givers	Amount Given 1967 through 1976 (billions $)	Percent of Total Given 1967 through 1976
Individuals	$188.1	86.5%
Foundations	18.9	8.7
Corporations	10.4	4.8
Total	$217.4*	100.0

Recipients	Amount Received 1967 through 1976 (billions $)	Percent of Total Received 1967 through 1976
Religion	$94.4	43.5%
Health	34.4	15.8
Education	33.1	15.2
Social Welfare	17.8	8.2
Arts and Humanities	9.9	4.6
Civic and Public	6.5	3.0
Other	21.0	9.7
Total	$217.1*	100.0

*Totals do not precisely agree because some figures for recent years are based on estimates by several different sources.
SOURCE: American Association of Fund-Raising Counsel, Inc.

WHO GIVES

Who donated the $217 billion that Americans gave away from 1967 through 1976? Huge, skyscraper-housed foundations? Big, multinational corporations? Actually, as the tabulation shows, foundations and corporations accounted for only 13.5 percent of the sum.

Individuals

The real givers—the big charitable spenders—were *individuals*. In 1976 alone, they gave $25.94 billion—88.2 percent of the amount given in that year. Individuals have historically set the pace, even if you go back nearly two decades. In 1961, for example, individuals gave $7.5 billion versus about $1.25 billion given by foundations and corporations; in 1965 the figures were about $10.0 billion versus $1.80 billion.

Of the $25.94 billion given by individuals in 1976, $23.58 billion was contributed by living donors and $2.36 billion by deceased donors through bequests. Again, this has been the pattern historically. In 1970, the figures were $14.40 billion from living donors versus $2.13 billion by bequest; in 1972, $16.84 versus $2.10; in 1974, $19.80 versus $2.07. Americans apparently agree with the 18th-century English religious writer L. M. Stretch who said: "Defer not charities till death. He that does so is rather liberal of another man's substance than his own."

Individuals contribute virtually all of the money received by American religious organizations, and they contribute about half of everything received by colleges and universities.

Other facts you should know about individual giving:

○ People are most supportive of those charities that offer specific, help-oriented services, and they are most hesitant about those that provide strictly educational or informational services (from a survey by the Gallup organization).
○ Even though people feel good about most voluntary social welfare and health organizations, they admit to knowing very little about them—what they do, services they offer, how much they spend, etc. (also from the Gallup survey).

○ According to a study by the Survey Research Center of the Institute for Social Research, University of Michigan: College graduates give six times as much as people with a grade school education; older people give more than the young—18- to 24-year-olds average $60 annually compared to $742 annually for people 75 and older; the married give more than the unmarried, rural residents more than city dwellers, the religious more than the unreligious, and the wealthy give a disproportionate amount. About 21 percent of all money from individual giving is donated by the one percent of United States households with annual incomes of $50,000 and more; the most donors, however—54 percent—come from households with annual incomes under $20,000.

○ Based on charitable contributions listed on 1973 federal income tax returns, the citizens of California give the most, followed by those of New York, Illinois and Pennsylvania.

Major bequests received in recent years include: $25 million to the University of Rochester (Charles F. Hutchison), about $10.5 million to Nova University (Leo Goodwin, Sr.), $8 million to the University of Cincinnati (William A. French), $7 million (art works) to the Metropolitan Museum of Art (Gertrude D. Walker), $5 million to the New Orleans Museum of Art (Victor K. Kiam), and $4 million to 14 different charities (Raymond A. Schulein).

Private Foundations

Since 1967 American foundations have increased their contributions in every year except 1973 and 1975:

Year	Amount Given (billions $)
1967	1.40
1968	1.60
1969	1.80
1970	1.90
1971	1.95
1972	2.00
1973	2.00
1974	2.11
1975	2.01
1976	2.13

SOURCE: American Association of Fund-Raising Counsel, Inc.

It is important to note, however, that the private foundations' *share* of total United States giving decreased from an average of 9.5 percent during 1966 through 1971 to 8.6 percent in 1973 and 7.2 percent in 1976. Factors accounting for this decline include: (1) Substantial increases in giving by individuals and corporations (corporate giving in 1976, for example, was up 15.4 percent over 1975), (2) poor stock market performance in 1973 and 1974, and (3) impact of the Tax Reform Act of 1969.

The giving priorities and interests of private foundations have remained uncannily constant over the years:

Number of Grants Given and Percent of
Foundation Total*

Field	1972	%	1973	%	1974	%	1975	%	1976	%
Education	2,204	23	1,979	36	2,278	28	2,372	26	2,852	29
Health	1,968	17	1,517	24	1,500	20	1,571	24	1,726	19
Sciences	1,221	16	1,153	12	1,510	12	2,006	16	2,285	17
Welfare	2,632	20	1,806	9	2,301	16	2,317	12	2,679	14
Humanities	836	8	715	8	1,038	11	1,200	9	892	9
Int'l Activities	784	12	656	9	679	11	883	11	1,350	11
Religion	781	4	179	2	290	2	329	2	335	1

*Based on reported grants of $10,000 or more in 1972 and $5,000 or more thereafter.
SOURCE: American Association of Fund-Raising Counsel, Inc.

Even as far back as 1921, private foundations were giving most heavily to education and health, and least to religion. It is reasonably safe to assume that these giving patterns will not change dramatically, although there may be some shifting of support from education to social causes (welfare).

A list of the 40 largest American private foundations, the amounts they gave in 1975 and 1976 and their fields of interest appears in Appendix A.

New Community Foundations

In recent years, community foundations have become a vital, influential force in foundation giving. By a large margin, they are the fastest growing segment of United States philanthropy. Community foundations work to maintain and up-grade community quality, especially in the social and cultural areas. Endowment funds from community members are administered by a representative board of community leaders. They are responsible for grant programs and charitable activities. Assets are managed by professionals—typically by trustee banks—and the public receives a regular report of finances and programs. Because community foundations qualify as "public charities," they are exempt from paying excise taxes and certain restrictions and requirements imposed on private foundations by the Tax Reform Act of 1969.

This helps to explain why the assets of community foundations have nearly doubled in the past 10 years. Today, the 219 United States community foundations have assets of over $1 billion and they give more than $70 million annually in their respective localities.

The giving interests of community foundations are somewhat similar to those of other foundations, but their priorities are quite different. While large private foundations give the most to education, followed by health, sciences, welfare and the humanities, the community foundations give the most (more than 35 percent) in the category of social welfare, followed by education, health, civic improvement, humanities and religion.

Community foundations are most prevalent in the Midwest, followed by New York, Pennsylvania and New England. The West Coast is developing many strong community foundations, and they are also gaining strength in the South and in Texas. There are relatively few community foundations in the western Plains and Mountain states. A listing of community foundations by locality appears in Appendix B.

According to the Council on Foundations, the 10 largest United States community foundations as of the end of fiscal year 1975 are as follows (figures in millions $):

Foundation Name	Assets	Grants
The Cleveland Foundation	179.8	8.6
The New York Community Trust	179.1	13.4
The Chicago Community Trust	91.6	4.9

Foundation Name	Assets	Grants
Committee of the Permanent Charity Fund, Inc. (Boston)	68.6	3.3
The San Francisco Foundation	44.5	4.2
The New Haven Foundation	31.4	1.7
Hartford Foundation for Public Giving	31.3	1.4
The Philadelphia Foundation	28.1	1.7
Kalamazoo Foundation	26.4	2.1
The Columbus Foundation	25.5	1.6

Corporations

If individuals are the bright stars in the philanthropic firmament, corporations are, by comparison, almost invisible on all but the clearest of nights. From 1960 through 1970, corporations contributed $8.2 billion or only 5.63 percent of the total given during that 11-year period. And in the most recent year for which figures are available—1976—corporations gave an even smaller share: $1.35 billion or 4.59 percent. This is not an indictment. As will be discussed in Chapter 5, corporations exist primarily to make a profit—not to give their stockholders' money away. This is true even in the face of some recent ambitious moves toward "corporate citizenship" and "enlightened corporate social consciousness." The problem is probably not the willingness of American business to support worthy causes, but rather the difficulty of creating a philanthropic distribution system that is fair, legal and socially correct. In addition, it should be recognized that the figures for corporate giving do not include the value of the time employees contribute on the job to charitable causes—a figure estimated to be in the billions annually.

Understandably, corporate giving is directly related to corporate profits. When profits rise, so do contributions (but not at the same rate). This is illustrated by this set of facts: (a) corporate profits in 1976 (estimated) were $147.8 billion compared to $114.5 billion (estimated) in 1975—a 29.1 percent increase; (b) corporate contributions in 1976 were a record $1.35 billion compared to $1.17 billion in 1975—a 15.4 percent increase. Conversely, when corporate profits drop, so do contributions (but, again, not at the same rate).

Under United States tax law, corporations are allowed to contribute up to five percent of their pretax net income to charity. Few, however, contribute the maximum amount. In 1969 corporations contributed an all-time high of 1.26 percent of their pretax net income to charity, but in the years since—with the exception of 1975—the trend has been downward. Corporations contributed only 0.91 percent (estimated) of their pretax income in 1976—close to the low for the previous 21 years of 0.86 percent (1956). Some legislative initiatives are underway to increase the allowable limit to 10 percent of pretax profits to encourage additional giving by those corporations now giving the allowable five percent.

Some observers, including most members of the Commission on Private Philanthropy and Public Needs, feel that corporations should give at least two percent of their pretax net income to charity. Many others, while not specifying an amount, feel that corporations should do much more than they are now doing. Given these views and the pressure of growing public opinion, and barring serious economic difficulties, the role of corporations in American philanthropy will probably increase in the years ahead.

One widespread idea about corporate giving is that the giant companies give a *proportionately* larger amount of their income to charity. Not true. Figures compiled by Anne Klepper* show that of 502 companies divided into 11 groups by size of assets—ranging from under $25 million to over $5 billion—the latter group gave the *smallest* percentage of their pretax net income to charity.

The figures on corporate giving for manufacturing and non-manufacturing companies, also compiled by Klepper,* are intriguing. For 1975, from top to bottom, they are as shown on the table on the following page.

---

* *Annual Survey of Corporate Contributions*, 1975, The Conference Board Report, 1977.

Manufacturing Companies

Industrial Classification	No. of Companies	Percent of Domestic Pretax Net Income Contributed
Rubber & misc. Plastic products	6	3.52
Printing and Publishing	6	1.98
Paper and like products	21	1.33
Textile Mill products	14	1.22
Mining	10	1.18
Machinery, nonelectrical	28	1.16
Fabricated Metal products	17	1.11
Pharmaceuticals	2	1.10
Primary Metal industries	12	0.98
Electrical Machinery and Equipment	19	0.97
Food, Beverage, Tobacco	24	0.91
Stone, Clay and Glass products	15	0.83
Transportation equipment	14	0.64
Chemicals and allied products	19	0.63
Petroleum and Gas	10	0.63

Nonmanufacturing Companies

Business services	15	2.12
Banking	82	1.48
Merchandising	16	1.16
Transportation companies	12	0.63
Engineering and Construction	9	0.58
Finance	5	0.42
Utilities	69	0.38
Telecommunications	16	0.30

The following tabulation shows how a large sampling of corporations divided their philanthropic support in three reasonably representative years:

Percent of Total & Total for Year (billions $)

Recipient	1972[a]	1974[b]	1975[c]
Health/Welfare	42.0%	38.5%	41.2%
Education	36.2	34.9	35.1

Percent of Total & Total for Year (billions $) – cont.

Recipient	1972[a]	1974[b]	1975[c]
Civic Groups	9.1	10.5	10.3
Culture/Art	4.1	7.3	7.6
Other			
(religion, economic,			
education, etc.)	8.5	8.8	5.8

[a]443 companies giving total of $322.6 million
[b]799 companies giving total of $438.1 million
[c]796 companies giving total of $436.8 million
SOURCE: The Conference Board.

WHO RECEIVES

As shown in the tabulation at the beginning of this chapter, six groups of charities received the $217.1 billion that Americans gave away from 1967 through 1976. Each group's share has remained remarkably the same over the years. Religion always leads by a huge margin, followed by Health, and then Education (these two are typically very close). Social Welfare, Arts and Humanities, Civic and Public, and "Other" follow in that order.

Religion

For where your treasure is,
there will your heart be also.
—MATTHEW 6:21

Religious organizations received 43.6 percent ($12.84 billion) of all funds contributed in 1976—a 9.9 percent increase over 1975. Historically, religion has received between 40 and 50+ percent of total United States philanthropic support. In 1960, for example, religion's share of total giving was 51.1 percent; in 1964, 49.4 percent; in 1967, 46.3 percent; in 1970, 43.2 percent, and in 1973, 43.1 percent.

Keep in mind that contributions to religious organizations are used in some down-to-earth ways. In fact, about one fifth goes for nonsacramental purposes. For example, in 1976 Roman Catholics in the United States operated 10,716 separate educational institutions, including 245 colleges and universities enrolling 432,597 students.

Figures on Protestant giving among 12 denominations are revealing and strongly suggest that those churches that stress tithing attract the highest average gift:

Membership, Total Contributions (millions), and Average Gift

Church	1972	1975
American Baptist Churches in the U.S.A.	1.4/$137.4/$93	1.6/$177.3/$110
American Lutheran Church	2.4/$184.9/$74	2.4/$247.5/$102
Church of the Nazarene	.417/$108.6/$260	1.441/$133.0/$301
Episcopal Church	3.0/$270.2/$88	2.8/$352.2/$124
Lutheran Church in America	3.0/$233.9/$77	2.9/$278.2/$93
Lutheran Church—Missouri Synod	2.7/$267.5/$96	2.7/$322.4/$117
Presbyterian Church in the U.S.	.946/$156.5/$165	.878/$189.0/$215
Seventh-Day Adventists	.449/$187.4/$417	.496/$256.7/$518
Southern Baptist Convention	12.0/$1.071/$89	12.7/$1.475/$116
United Church of Christ	1.9/$193.3/$102	1.8/$225.6/$124
United Methodist Church	10.1/$885.7/$87	9.9/$1.009/$101
United Presbyterian Church in the U.S.A.	2.9/$372.1/$128	2.6/$451.3/$170

SOURCE: *Yearbook of American and Canadian Churches*, 1974, 1975, 1976. © 1974, 1975, 1976 by The National Council of the Churches of Christ in the USA. Used by permission of Abingdon Press.

Health

Of the $4.37 billion given for health purposes in 1976, the American Association of Fund-Raising Counsel, Inc. estimates that $1.2 billion went for personal health care; $1 billion to local, regional and national health agencies to be used in a variety of ways; $900 million to endow health institutions; $700 million to construct and equip health facilities; $220 million to medical research, and $280 million and $70 million to the United Way and Red Cross respectively to meet many different health needs.

A comparison of how the philanthropic health dollar has been distributed over a recent four-year period shows that most of it always goes for personal health care and—somewhat disconcertingly—least of it for medical research:

	1973	1974	1975	1976
Personal Health Care	$1.2 bil	1.0 bil	1.1 bil	1.2 bil
Health Agencies	$835 mil	910 mil	930 mil	1.0 bil
Endowments	$780 mil	825 mil	870 mil	900 mil
Construct./Equip.	$730 mil	775 mil	705 mil	700 mil
Research	$220 mil	220 mil	225 mil	220 mil
United Way	$135 mil	145 mil	116 mil	280 mil
Red Cross	$ 20 mil	21 mil	—	70 mil

SOURCE: American Association of Fund-Raising Counsel, Inc.

The steady increase in contributions to endow health institutions is explained by the growing popularity of deferred giving. The marked decrease in contributions to construct and equip health facilities is attributable to the growing governmental role in hospital financing.

The leading national volunteer health agencies in recent years are as follows (figures in millions $):

Agency	1969	1973	1976
American Cancer Society, Inc.	61.0	93.0	118.9
American Heart Association	41.0	54.5	66.7
The National Foundation	22.6	42.7	55.0
American Lung Association	38.5	39.3	41.1
National Easter Seal Society for Crippled Children and Adults	23.3	34.4	40.9*
Muscular Dystrophy Association, Inc.	9.8	20.6	37.4
National Association for Retarded Citizens	18.0*	22.6	27.2*
United Cerebral Palsy Association, Inc.	13.3	18.1	19.5
National Multiple Sclerosis Society	7.4	12.1	19.0*
Planned Parenthood Foundation of America, Inc.	15.9	20.7	18.0*
Mental Health Association	9.9	13.7	15.8*
The Arthritis Foundation	8.1	10.7	13.1*
Leukemia Society of America, Inc.	2.5*	6.4	9.4
Cystic Fibrosis Foundation	4.2	7.0	9.1*
American Diabetes Association, Inc.	—	1.6	6.6*
National Kidney Foundation, Inc.	2.1	5.6	6.1*
National Hemophilia Foundation	2.2	3.5	4.8*

Agency	1969	1973	1976
Epilepsy Foundation of America	3.1	4.5	4.6*
National Society for the Prevention of Blindness, Inc.	1.9	2.7	3.7*
American Foundation for the Blind, Inc.	4.7	2.3	3.2
National Council on Alcoholism	2.2*	2.6	3.0*
Recording for the Blind, Inc.	.8	1.3	2.1*
Damon Runyon-Walter Winchell Cancer Fund, Inc.	2.0	1.5	1.6

*Estimated

SOURCE: American Association of Fund-Raising Counsel, Inc.

Major gifts to health causes in recent years include: $49.7 million to the Henry Ford Hospital (Ford Foundation); $15 million to the National Academy of Sciences (Robert Wood Johnson Foundation); $7 million+ to the Robert Packer Hospital (Emily Baker Guthrie); $2.6 million to The Johns Hopkins School of Medicine (William Penn Foundation); $2.5 million to the Memorial Sloan-Kettering Cancer Center (Mrs. Abby Rockefeller Mauze); and $2.5 million to the Columbia Presbyterian Medical Center (Kresge Foundation).

Education

From 1970 through 1976, contributions to education from all sources increased by an average annual rate of 6.6 percent and the total received was $24.85 billion. Contributions to education in 1976 alone totaled $4.07 billion—a jump of 13.4 percent over the previous year and a record high of 13.8 percent of all funds contributed that year. It should be noted, however, that contributions to education in 1975 were down by 3.5 percent compared to 1974—the only decrease to occur from 1960 through 1976.

Historically, higher education has received over half of all contributions to education, with the balance earmarked for elementary and secondary schools, independent institutions (military and boarding schools, for example) and a range of other institutions. Many of these are church-related. Of the amount given annually to education from 1969 through 1976, *higher* education's share has fluctuated significantly—from a low of 56.4 percent in 1971 to a high of 60.3 percent in 1974.

The six traditional sources of support for higher education have remained fairly constant over the years, as the following tabulation shows:*

Percent of Total Support Given by Source
and Total Received (Billions $) from All Sources

Source of Support	1970–71		1973–74		1975–76	
Nonalumni	26.6		24.8		23.6	
Alumni	24.6		22.7		24.4	
Foundations	22.5	$1.86	23.9	$2.24	22.8	$2.41
Business	13.9		15.8		15.7	
Religion	5.6		5.2		5.4	
Other	6.8		7.6		8.1	

SOURCE: Council for Financial Aid to Education.

The year 1976 marked the fifth consecutive year that corporations increased their giving to higher education, even though corporate profits were off by 10 percent in 1975.

Harvard led major colleges and universities in gifts and bequests received in 1976 with over $59 million. Among smaller colleges and universities, Stevens Institute of Technology led with $8.3 million. A complete listing of higher educational institutions attracting the most philanthropic support from 1969 through 1976 appears in Appendix C.

Major gifts to education in recent years include: $23 million to Harvard Medical School (Monsanto Chemical Company); $14 million to the California Institute of the Arts (Disney Foundation); $7 million to the University of Rochester (Eastman Kodak Company); $7 million to the Philadelphia College of Art (Atlantic Richfield Company); $5 million to Baylor Medical College (Houston Endowment); and $4.4 million to the Colorado School of Mines (Brown Foundation).

Social Welfare

Americans gave $2.67 billion for social welfare in 1976—an 8.5 percent increase over 1975—which accounted for 9.1 per-

---

*Based on a survey involving an average of 1,026 institutions.

cent of all charitable contributions. The 9.1 percent figure represents the first decrease in social welfare's share of American philanthropy since 1968.

Social welfare agencies are concerned with fostering the quality of many different aspects of American community life. They include Boy Scouts of America, Girl Scouts of the U.S.A., Boys' Clubs of America, Salvation Army, USO, Urban League, Travelers Aid, American Red Cross and YMCA/ YWCA.

Unquestionably, the United Way is the dominant force in raising funds for such agencies. In 1976 the United Way conducted 2,307 campaigns in the United States and Canada. Over 37 million individuals, groups and corporations contributed. United States receipts exceeded $1.1 billion for the first time, and overhead averaged only 4.7 percent of all contributions.

The United Way does more than raise money: It helps to rally support for social welfare from many different community elements. It also works with member agencies and community leaders to plan for optimum use of all of the funds that are raised.

Ever wonder how much each United Way agency receives? Here is a look at the allocation of funds in 1975/1976:

Allocation of United Way Funds (percent)

Agency	1975/1976
American Red Cross	14.8%
Boy Scouts of America	5.4
Boys' Clubs of America	4.4
Family Service, Nondenominational	7.0
Girl Scouts of the U.S.A.	3.2
Home Health Agency	3.0
Hospitals	4.4
Salvation Army	5.0
Settlement House/Neighborhood Center	6.1
Urban League-Local	2.3
YMCA	6.2
YWCA	4.0

SOURCE: American Association of Fund-Raising Counsel, Inc.

Major gifts to social welfare in recent years include: $2.3 million to the National Urban League (Ford Foundation); $1.6 million to the St. John Urban Renewal Program of the City of Flint, Michigan (Charles Stewart Mott Foundation); and $1 million to the Urban Institute (Ford Foundation).

Catholic, Jewish and Protestant religious groups have also been important sources of support for welfare agencies in recent years. The Council of Jewish Federations and Welfare Funds reported, for example, that from 1974 through 1976 it raised more than $1.6 billion in pledges.

Arts and Humanities

About $2.08 billion was given to the arts and humanities in 1976—a 7.2 percent increase over 1975—which represented 7.1 percent of all contributions. This area was up significantly from 1973 when it received only about 5.1 percent of total funds given.

The National Endowment for the Arts and Humanities—a federally funded program—is an important, steady source of support. In 1976, for example, $89.5 million was available from this source for grants to arts organizations. In addition, the Arts, Humanities and Cultural Affairs Act of 1976 made $18 million available in 1978 for matching by the private sector—a major incentive.

Nevertheless, most support for the arts and humanities will probably continue to come from the traditional sources—individuals, corporations, foundations and earned income. In recent years, individuals have been the main source of support. Corporations have also taken an active role. One study, conducted by The Conference Board in December of 1976, shows that museums were most popular with corporations, followed by public television and radio. Least popular: cultural centers and theaters.

Major gifts to cultural causes in recent years include: $10–$15 million (objects of Asian art) to the Asian Society (John D. Rockefeller III); $10 million to National Gallery of Art (Andrew W. Mellon Foundation); $8.5 million to American Academy of Arts and Sciences (Rowland Foundation); $7.3

million (art works) to Metropolitan Museum of Art (Emma Sheafer); $5 million to Indiana Museum of Art (Krannert Charitable Trust); and $2.9 million to Indiana State Symphony (Lilly Endowment).

Civic and Public Affairs

Contributions to civic and public affairs increased by 37 percent from 1974 to 1976—a direct result of spending for the United States Bicentennial. The amount given in 1976 alone was $970 million—an 18.2 percent increase over 1975—which was 3.3 percent of all funds given.

Probably because they perceived them as noncontroversial and rich in public relations potential, corporations responded warmly to Bicentennial projects. Many sponsored contests with cash awards. Others donated cash, employee time and materials to construct exhibits, displays, floats and other projects to celebrate the nation's 200th birthday.

Individuals and foundations also responded. DeWitt Wallace, founder of the *Reader's Digest* Association, Inc., gave $4 million to build a theater in Colonial Williamsburg, and the Lilly Endowment gave $3,750,000 to help restore and operate Historic New Harmony, Inc.

Other major gifts to civic causes in recent years include: $3.5 million to the Square Mountain resort area in Maine (Scott Paper Company); $3.5 million to Boise, Idaho, for a performing arts center (Harry Morrison Family Foundation); $2.8 million to the National Council on Crime and Delinquency (Grace Hodgson Flandrau); $2.5 million to the city of New York for a new Department of Cultural Affairs (Gulf & Western Industries); $1.8 million to the New York Botanical Garden (Mary Flagler Cary Charitable Trust); and $1.8 million to the Dallas Public Library (Mrs. Virginia Lazenby O'Hara).

Because many of the causes involved in the Bicentennial-linked contributions are of continuing concern (historic preservation, municipal and community improvement, ecology, housing), it is reasonable to assume that civic and public affairs will continue to attract significant philanthropic support from all giving sources.

Other

This category encompasses contributions made principally in response to disasters, such as floods and earthquakes. About $2.42 billion was given for such purposes in 1976—8.2 percent of all giving and a 1.7 percent increase over 1975.

HOW CONTRIBUTIONS ARE MADE

The "how" of corporate and foundation giving can be quickly covered. Corporations give in cash, services and materials—but mostly in cash. Foundations give cash almost exclusively. In contrast, individuals give in many different ways, all of which are influenced by federal and state tax laws.

Individual giving can be divided into two broad categories: gifts made during life and gifts by will (upon death). The information that follows is designed only to *introduce* you to *some* of the mechanics of individual giving. The intent is to give you an awareness-level understanding of the major ways in which people give. Complete details, impact of state laws, qualifying statements and footnotes (of which there are many), new Internal Revenue Service rulings, changes made beyond the Tax Reform Act of 1976 and other important data are not included. They are well beyond the scope of this section. *Consequently, it is extremely important that you seek legal counsel when you address these matters and relate them to real-life prospects and gifts.*

Gifts Made During Life

Outright Gifts of Money.   Most individual giving takes this form. It is direct and uncomplicated. It typically involves dropping a quarter into a supermarket campaign cannister, or a $5 bill onto the church collection plate, or a check into the mail to one's alma mater. Increasingly, such giving is being done automatically—by payroll deduction to United Way, for example.

A donor who gives cash to qualifying organizations (schools, hospitals, churches and other publicly supported charities) can deduct his gift on his federal income tax return. He can claim deductions for such gifts up to 50 percent of his adjusted gross income. If he gives over the 50 percent ceiling, he can deduct the excess for the next five years until it is used up (the 50 percent ceiling applies in each carryover year). A donor who makes a cash contribution receives another benefit: He reduces his estate and, therefore, his estate tax.

Appreciated Securities and Real Estate. If the contributed property (stock, house, farm, etc.) has been held for more than one year,* the donor receives two important tax benefits: (1) Charitable deduction for the present fair market value of his gift, and (2) avoidance of capital gains tax payable on the appreciation if he had sold the property. The deductibility ceiling for such gifts is 30 percent of adjusted gross income, with a five-year/30 percent carryover privilege for any surplus. Donors who give appreciated property held for less than one year receive a charitable deduction only for the cost-basis of the property—not for its appreciated value. The deductibility ceiling for such gifts is 50 percent of adjusted gross income with a five-year/50 percent carryover privilege. A donor who gives appreciated property reduces his estate and, therefore, the federal and state tax on it.

EXAMPLE: Mr. Winslow gives his alma mater stock for which he paid $5,000 six years ago and which is now worth $15,000. He gets a $15,000 charitable deduction and completely avoids capital gains tax on the $10,000 appreciation.

Appreciated Art Works, Other Personal Property. Paintings, coin collections, books, and other tangible property is commonly given to charitable organizations. If the property's use relates directly to the receiving charity's function (such as a painting given to a publicly supported art museum), the donor can deduct the item's full fair market value and not be subject to capital gains tax on the appreciation. The deductibility ceiling for such gifts is 30 percent of adjusted gross income, with a five-year/30 percent carryover privilege for any surplus. If the property given by the donor does not relate to the charity's exempt function, the donor may deduct only the cost-basis of the property plus one half of its appreciation.

---

*The one-year requirement applies to property purchased after March 31, 1977.

EXAMPLE: Mrs. Cooper paid $10,000 for a painting several years ago, and it is now worth $40,000. By donating it to an art museum, she qualifies for a $40,000 deduction. If, however, she had donated it to an organization for a use not related to the organization's exempt function, her deduction would be reduced to $25,000.

Life Insurance.   Gifts of life insurance typically take this form: Mr. Jones decides he has more life insurance than he needs. Rather than cancel one of his policies, he gives it to his church. He also gives his church an amount equal to the annual premium on the policy. Mr. Jones can deduct the current fair market value of the policy on his federal income tax return plus the amount he gives annually to pay the premium. Unless Mr. Jones dies within three years of the date he gave the policy to his church, the policy proceeds will not be part of his estate for federal estate tax purposes. Even if the policy proceeds were included in his estate, they would not be taxable because of his offsetting charitable deduction.

Life Income Agreements (Deferred Gifts).   These are growing in popularity because they make it possible for individuals to: (a) give to charity, (b) receive a lifetime income, and (c) receive substantial tax benefits. There are several types of life income agreements and many variations of each type. Five of the most common are briefly described below.

Annuity Trust.   Mr. Swenson transfers appreciated securities into a trust. He receives from the trust a fixed dollar amount each year for as long as he lives. He gets the same amount each year regardless of whether the trust income increases or decreases. When he dies, the assets remaining in the trust become the property of the charity designated in the trust agreement. In addition to helping the charity of his choice, Mr. Swenson: (1) Avoids the capital gains tax he would have had to pay had he sold the appreciated securities, (2) receives a charitable contribution deduction for part of the value of the securities which will probably reduce his income taxes for several years and probably increase his spendable income, and (3) receives regular income from the trust.

Unitrust.   This agreement has many of the same features and advantages as the Annuity Trust. Its principal difference is that the payout to the donor or income beneficiary is variable. It is based on a fixed percentage (at least five percent) of the fair market value of the trust assets, *as valued annually*. Consequently, if the trust assets increase in value, the income beneficiary receives correspondingly larger payments. In some situations, this will provide a hedge against inflation. If the trust assets decrease in a given year, the income beneficiary still receives the stated percentage. The deficit is covered by capital gains or principal.

Gift Annuity. Basically, this is an arrangement whereby a donor transfers money or securities to the charity of his choice in return for the charity's promise to pay him an agreed-upon income for his lifetime. The amount of income the donor gets depends upon his age at the time he makes the gift. Benefits include: (1) Charitable contribution deduction on federal income tax return. (The deductibility ceiling is 50 percent of adjusted gross income if the annuity is funded with money, and 30 percent of adjusted gross income if it is funded with long-term appreciated securities. Under some circumstances, the 30 percent ceiling can be raised to 50 percent. Five-year carryover privileges apply in each case); (2) income that may be largely tax free (donor's age is the determining factor), (3) reduced capital gains taxes if the annuity is funded with appreciated securities, and (4) reduction of federal estate tax.

Deferred Payment Gift Annuity. This is the same as the Gift Annuity except that the donor defers receipt of the annuity income until he needs it most—usually, upon retirement. Another important advantage: The donor is entitled to take the charitable contribution deduction (for part of the value of the property) immediately—when his income is relatively high and the deduction generates maximum income tax savings.

Pooled Income Fund. This agreement enables a donor of limited means to give to charity and—as with the other agreements—receive lifetime income. Assume, for example, that Dr. Todd gives $12,000 to a fund for the benefit of his local Boys' Club. Dr. Todd's gift is put into a common investment account (pooled income fund) together with gifts from other participating donors. Dr. Todd and the others receive dividends from the fund annually. After Dr. Todd and his wife die, the Boys' Club will receive the $12,000. While they are alive, the Todds receive income tax benefits (they qualify for a charitable deduction for the discounted value of the $12,000). There will also be estate tax benefits (only Mrs. Todd's life interest will be taxed in Dr. Todd's estate).

Gifts by Will

In a typical gift by will (bequest), Mr. Orton, a single man, leaves $40,000 to Mercy Hospital. The balance of his estate goes to two nephews. If Mr. Orton's total estate is $300,000, the estate tax will be reduced by $12,640, making the actual "cost" of the gift not $40,000, but $27,360.

Individuals give by bequest in a variety of other ways. Here are two examples:

○ Mr. Casey leaves his entire $200,000 estate in a charitable Annuity Trust. His brother, Harold, is to receive a set amount annually from the trust. When Harold dies, the trust ends and the principal goes to Mr. Casey's favorite charity. Mr. Casey's estate will receive a large estate tax deduction. The amount of the deduction will depend on how much money it is predicted that Harold will receive before he dies (government tables are used to make this calculation). The balance remaining in the trust is the charity's share and is deductible from Mr. Casey's estate as a charitable contribution.

○ By means of two trusts, Mr. Stanley leaves his entire estate to Mrs. Stanley. When Mrs. Stanley dies, the principal of one of the trusts is distributed as her will directs. The principal of the other trust goes to the American Heart Association. Benefits: There is no federal estate tax on Mr. Stanley's estate, and Mrs. Stanley's estate may also escape federal estate tax. The explanation is involved, but it centers on the fact that half of Mr. Stanley's estate qualified for an estate tax "marital deduction," and the other half has been placed in a charitable unitrust. The latter doesn't qualify for the marital deduction, but much of it does qualify for a charitable deduction. Consequently, the amount left in the estate subject to federal estate tax is greatly reduced.

Chapter Two

MAKING THE MOST OF THE HUMAN NEED TO GIVE

To succeed in fund-raising, you must acquire a working knowledge of the forces that motivate people to give. Be fore-warned, however: Even in acts of charity, selflessness does not rule the day. The fact is, human beings give their wealth to other human beings for seven basic reasons or combina-tions thereof, all of which are at least in part self-fulfilling. This is a practical, not a cynical, assessment.

RELIGIOUS BELIEFS

Some individuals make gifts because the teachings of their religion direct them to do so, and because they seek the spiri-tual and temporal rewards promised to the obedient. Biblical injunctions to give to the poor and needy abound in the Old and New Testaments. In his instructions to Moses on Mount Sinai, the Lord tells his people to relieve a brother "fallen in decay" and to "Take thou no usury of him . . ." (Leviticus 25: 35, 36). Amos and Micah issue a clear call for justice for the poor. And Moses commanded the Israelites to "open thine hand wide unto thy brother, to thy poor, and to thy needy. . . ." (Deuteronomy 15:11).

The story of the Good Samaritan is representative of New Testament teachings about charity. You will recall that a certain man traveling from Jerusalem to Jericho "fell among thieves" (Luke 10:30) and was, in effect, mugged and left to die. A priest and a Levite passed him by, but a "certain Samaritan . . . had compassion on him, bound up his wounds . . . set him on his own beast, and brought him to an inn, and took care of him" (Luke 10:33, 34). Unquestionably, those were charitable acts, but the Samaritan went further: "And on the morrow when he departed, he took out two pence, and gave them to the host [innkeeper] and said unto him, Take care of him: and whatsoever thou spendest more, when I come again, I will repay thee" (Luke 10:35).

Paul said that every man should give ungrudgingly, "for God loveth a cheerful giver" (2 Corinthians, 9:7). Paul also told his followers to labor with their hands so that they could "give to him that needeth" (Ephesians 4:28).

Other great religious movements, especially those of the East, repeatedly implore help for the poor and needy. Buddhism, for example, stresses compassion for suffering; Islam, the responsibility of the wealthy to the disadvantaged.

GUILT

There can be little doubt that feelings of guilt—justified or unjustified—are factors in a significant number of philanthropic gifts. This is especially true in modern America, where the plight of the underprivileged has received comprehensive public exposure. Through the searching eye of television, millions of Americans have been made painfully aware of Appalachian poverty, migrant worker malnutrition, and the horrors of Negro slavery. In fact, some sociologists now speak routinely of "mass guilt complexes."

It is also reasonably safe to assume that the larger the gift, the greater the likelihood that guilt feelings motivated it. Why? Because in a society of haves and have-nots, the accumulation of great wealth—whether inherited, honestly earned or stolen—inevitably gives rise to feelings of guilt. If pressed on this point, donors will deny it. This response is understandable, not merely because it is a common defensive reaction, but also because guilt feelings often go unrecognized by the individuals who harbor them. When people give their money to charity, they have reason to believe that they are benefiting society. That knowledge helps to relieve their guilt feelings.[1]

Guilt as a motivating factor in giving is directly in evidence in the "conscience funds" maintained by many police forces. Individuals can anonymously make restitution for unpunished wrongs through such funds. A common pattern is for middle-aged people to send in checks to pay for crimes committed in their youth.[2]

Reputable fund-raisers recognize the role guilt plays in giving but they are circumspect about using it. They know that exploiting a prospective donor's guilt feelings will not build mutual trust and respect. They also know that such tactics are not conducive to a successful long-term cultivation and fund-raising program in the community of which they are a part.

RECOGNITION

Man longs for immortality. The giving of gifts to which one's name is attached is one way to achieve at least a degree of immortality. One Greek donor of long ago was refreshingly candid on this subject. He requested that his gift be reported on at least three marble tablets: ". . . so that to citizens and non-citizens alike . . . my philanthropic and kindly act may be evident and well known . . . my idea is to achieve immortality in making such a just and kindly disposal."[3]

The list of Americans who have followed the Greek's example is long and well known. Their names also appear on marble tablets—attached to buildings: Stanford University, Carnegie Free Public Library, Whitney Museum, Wrigley Field. The list goes on.

The names of other donors who wanted to be remembered are associated with important prizes (Pulitzer, Nobel); with scholarships and fellowships (Rhodes, Danforth); and with thousands of programs, institutes, swimming pools, centers, clinics, museums, parks, laboratories, art galleries, hospitals —you name it—across the country.

While no conclusive research has been done on the subject, the number of donors who give anonymously—and thus clearly signal that they do not want recognition—is probably fewer than 10 in 100. Too, at least some of those who give anonymously do so not for reasons of modesty, but to avoid the public exposure that could send flocks of fund-raisers to their doorsteps.

You must openly and honestly recognize the ego needs of prospective donors—and, where practical, accommodate them. If an individual, as a condition of making a gift, wants his name attached to it, that is his right. All such gifts, however, should be approved by the president or governing board of the receiving institution before commitments of any kind are made to the donor. In some circumstances, institutions would clearly compromise their principles by accepting the money and names of certain donors—for example, persons who are known to be inimical to the recipient's ethics and goals.

Every institution would do well to delineate clearly its policy on naming buildings, rooms, programs, etc. Among the questions to be resolved is this one: What percentage of the total cost of a building (or room or program) must a donor contribute in order for it to be named after him? The figure arrived at is less important than establishing a written policy on the matter. Obviously, though, no building, room, or program should be "sold" to a donor for anything less than a "controlling interest" in it—51 percent or more.

Because of the importance of recognition to many donors, always ask them if they want publicity. Even if they say no, they will appreciate your thoughtfulness in raising the question. If they say yes, you should work closely with your institution's public relations office or news bureau, or directly with the local press to see that the donors' desires are met. And here's a helpful followup suggestion: Send donors press clippings with a cover letter thanking them for their contribution.

In most cases it is in your interest to give donors public recognition. Such publicity not only draws favorable attention to your cause, but it also applies social pressure on others to contribute—particularly the wealthy. Most of us have watched TV fund-raising marathons in which, say, Bill Stubbs, a bowler in the All-City League, calls in with a $20 pledge and challenges all other bowlers to match it. Bill is applying social pressure. But the fact is, the technique is effective with big donors, too. When you publicize the $100,000 gift of Mr. Blank, Elmville's well-known real estate developer, you and Mr. Blank in effect challenge others in Mr. Blank's income bracket to give a comparable gift. In short, the desire to keep up with the Joneses is a philanthropic fact of life, and publicity is an excellent way for you to capitalize on it.

SELF-PRESERVATION AND FEAR

Some people give to charity in an effort to save themselves—from hell, from disease, from militant minority groups—from anything that they believe threatens their survival.

Fear of hell comes through with unforgettable force in the opening lines of a will cited by Courtney Kenney, an English critic of charities: "For the benefit of my poor soul, God help me, as a kind of atonement for the great crimes I have committed against the commandments of God, I do award. . . ."[4]

National health campaigns capitalize on Americans' fear of certain diseases—and on the promise of cures. Do any of these sound familiar? "We're Fighting For Your Life"— "Money Walks: Give to Easter Seals"—"Conquer Cancer with a Check and a Checkup"—"A Massive, Unprecedented Human Tragedy Is In the Making"—"Diabetes: To Most It's Just a Word; to Some It's a Way of Life."

If you doubt that health fund-raisers play on people's fears, consider the results of the 1976 American Cancer Society and American Heart Association campaigns. Cancer raised $118.8 million compared to $66.6 million for heart, despite the fact that heart disease claims more than three times as many lives as cancer. Logically, heart should have outpulled cancer, but the fact is that people *perceive* cancer as the greater threat. This was confirmed by a survey released early in 1977 which showed that cancer was the disease Americans feared above all others.

In the late 1960's, many whites who lived in cities that

experienced black rioting made financial contributions to black causes. While some of the donors were responding to an awakened awareness of the blacks' plight, others were simply buying protection. In fact, some militant blacks "solicited" contributions precisely along these lines.

When war broke out between Egypt and Israel in 1967, the American Jewish community responded with a remarkable outpouring of aid funds for their homeland. At a meeting in the Waldorf-Astoria Hotel on the day fighting began, New York Jews pledged $1 million a minute during one quarter-hour period. And within the week, Jews nationwide had given $90 million. Many of the donors redeemed life insurance policies, went into debt, and sold their cars.[5] Self-preservation—in its broadest and noblest sense—is very much in evidence in this fund-raising accomplishment.

TAX REWARDS

Many Americans believe that philanthropic giving is motivated above all else by tax considerations. Unquestionably, the Internal Revenue Code offers special tax deductions, exclusions and exemptions to those who give. Under these circumstances, gifts—especially when given by the very wealthy—cost donors only a fraction of their face value.

Nevertheless, it is not safe to assume that taxes are a major consideration in giving. According to a University of Michigan survey, only at the $100,000-plus level do more than 50 percent of donors cite taxes as a major factor. Only one taxpayer in five knows, even roughly, how much in taxes each added dollar of deductions will save. And only 12 times in thousands of interviews did people offer tax reasons for changing their giving.[6] Furthermore, the Fund-Raising Institute claims that donors rate tax considerations as 10th or later in priority.[7]

Bear in mind, too, that philanthropic giving thrived long before income tax laws. For example, Rockefeller, Carnegie, and Stanford made huge gifts with no tax incentives whatsoever.[8] And today many organizations receive substantial contributions, even though they are non-tax-exempt. This means, of course, that those who support them do not qualify for charitable income tax deductions.

When you offer a prospective donor a tax deduction as an incentive for giving, you offer him nothing unique: Thousands of other tax-exempt institutions offer precisely the same thing. The moral here is do not oversell tax angles; rather, sell the worthiness of your institution to receive a contribution and its ability to use it with maximum effectiveness. The time to talk about tax rewards is *after* your prospect is sold on your institution or project. This strategy is important for another reason: It enables the prospect to maintain his integrity. He doesn't want to come across to you as someone whose overriding interest is saving taxes.

OBLIGATION

We have all seen headlines like these: "Immigrant Gives Priceless Paintings to White House"—"Grateful Patient Leaves Fortune to Hospital"—"Harvard Grad Establishes Endowed Chair"—"Oil Tycoon Bequeaths Estate to Secretary."

These donors are giving, at least in part, out of a sense of obligation or a feeling of indebtedness. Their quoted statements invariably read like this: "I wanted to do something to pay back my alma mater for all that it did for me," or "I'm alive today because of Midtown Hospital and its doctors and nurses."

In some cases, donors who give out of a sense of obligation are also giving to achieve recognition. The former simply provides a socially acceptable "cover" for the latter.

Obligation as a fund-raising technique has been used most frequently—and infamously—in direct mail campaigns. Remember the Ident-o-tag? It was the miniature license plate for key chains sent out in the millions by the Disabled American Veterans. You didn't ask for it. It simply arrived, uninvited, each year in your mail box. The Ident-o-tag strategy was to make the recipient feel obligated to contribute. It worked: In 1971 alone, the Ident-o-tag raised nearly $21 million for the DAV![9]

For sheer bad taste, however, the Ident-o-tag must move over for a technique widely employed in the early 1970's by a religious sect. Their *modus operandi* involved stationing college-age girls in airports serving large cities. The girls would rush up to travelers—males made the best targets—and pin a carnation on them, then gush something like, "A handsome carnation for a handsome man." With the carnation—and the compliment—firmly secured, an appeal for funds followed. It invariably succeeded.

The most important thing to remember about obligation as a factor in giving is that it must originate naturally with the prospective donor. You cannot create it, and you should not try.

PRESSURE

By and large, you cannot control the factors described above in this chapter that influence giving. You can turn them to your advantage if they exist naturally, but you cannot control them. Fortunately, that is not true of pressure.

Professional fund-raisers may react with alarm to the author's use of the word "pressure." Some would say that it is appropriately applied to certain used-car-lot operations but not to properly established and managed philanthropic organizations. They would prefer "marketing," "salesmanship," or even "education." They may be right, and consequently it is important for you to understand that "pressure" as used herein is not meant in any negative sense. It is meant, rather, in this sense: In the final analysis, the fund-raiser must confront the prospect and ask for a contribution, and this act—in and of itself—constitutes "pressure."

By their very nature, personal appeals or even telephone appeals for contributions involve pressure and are extremely difficult for most people to resist. Such appeals have an especially high probability of success when they are made on a one-to-one basis by respected, well-known community or public figures. The services of a respected basketball coach, for example, in a telephone campaign to raise college athletic funds can prove invaluable. What UCLA alumnus could have turned down an appeal from Johnny Wooden at the height of his coaching career?

Social pressure to give can be downright devastating in certain situations. Can you resist, for example, adding to the church collection plate when those to your left, right, rear and front are giving—and watching? And can you resist the plea of a bright-eyed high school girl and her comely companion to buy a paper poppy in, say, downtown Denver?

Some fund-raising campaigns involving kits that pass from neighbor to neighbor make exceptionally effective use of peer pressure. For example, the 1977 Easter Seal fund-raising kit featured a large, sturdy envelope with a flap on which were printed the column headings "Name," "Address," and "Amt." Recipients of the kit were instructed to deposit their contribution, fill in the information on the flap, and then "pass this kit to your neighbor right away." The instructions to volunteers in charge of circulating the kits were especially direct:

"You may wish to make your own gift first. This will make it easier for others to give. Write your name, address, and amount on Line 1 on the kit flap. (Experience shows that the larger your gift, the larger will be your neighbors' gifts. Please set the pace!)"

Churches that hold "cake auctions" and similar events also make skillful use of peer pressure. One church raised over $500 for a new organ by inviting mothers and daughters to bake and decorate cakes for a "most original cake" contest. The cakes were then auctioned off to the highest bidders—usually fathers and grandfathers—at a well-attended church anniversary party. Paternal pride carried the day!

Although you may wish it were otherwise, pressure is essential in raising money. Just as you cannot make an omelet without breaking eggs, you cannot raise money without applying pressure. You must believe enough in your cause to ask directly, forcefully and convincingly. You must use the most influential people available to you: the mayor of your city, director of your hospital, president of your college, leader of your church. And you must *never* apologize. True, you will probably offend someone at some point along the way. One fund-raising pro shrugs this off with the observation, "The dogs bark, but the caravan moves on." He recognizes—and you should, too—that a fund-raiser is bound to suffer difficulties en route to his goal, but if he persists they are not likely to stop his forward progress. You should also recognize that you will flatter more people than you will offend, especially if you ask for handsome sums and involve attractive, popular personalities in the process.

People who sincerely believe in the correctness of their cause are pleasantly bold about asking. They honestly believe that their cause is worthy of people's financial support. But more than that, they believe that the *donors themselves* will benefit in at least two ways by giving to them: (1) They will be publicly identifying themselves with a respected, worthwhile cause—a move that will inevitably be helpful to them; and (2) they will receive great personal satisfaction—inner peace, if you will—from the knowledge that they are helping to further that cause.

This chapter has dealt with the identifiable, measurable, predictable factors that motivate acts of charity. Some of what has been said may come across as callous, and you may well ask, "But don't some people give out of goodness and decency—out of a sincere desire to help?" Yes, they do. Some people are charitable in the purest, most spiritual sense of the word. They give because they love mankind, because they are sensitive to the suffering of others, because they truly want to share what they have with those who have less. If you stay in fund-raising very long, you will meet these noble people. And if you are patient and observant, they will rekindle your faith in mankind and increase your own capacity to give and love.

NOTES

1. Gerald S. Soroker, *Fund Raising for Philanthropy* (Pittsburgh: Pittsburgh Jewish Publication and Education Foundation, 1974), p. 18.
2. George G. Kirstein, *Better Giving: The New Needs of American Philanthropy* (Boston: Houghton Mifflin Company, 1975), p. 5.
3. Benedict Nightingale, *Charities* (London: Allen Lane, 1973), p. 103.
4. Ibid., p. 124.
5. *Time*, June 16, 1967.
6. *Wall Street Journal*, June 11, 1975.
7. *Tips of the Month*, Fund-Raising Institute, Third Edition.
8. George G. Kirstein, op. cit., p. 8.
9. Harvey Katz, *GIVE! Who Gets Your Charity Dollar?* (Garden City, New York: Anchor Press, 1974), p. 124.

Chapter Three
_____

BEFORE YOU ASK

Fund-raising is a lot like house painting: Most of the work and some of the greatest challenges are in *preparing* to do the job, rather than in the job itself. This chapter takes you through the preparatory steps that are indispensable to effective solicitation.

ESTABLISHING THE CAUSE

Not surprisingly, America's most successful political campaigns have been keyed to causes—to well-articulated, pressing public concerns often expressed in labels or declarations: "The New Frontier"; "The Great Society"; "Let us reason together"; "We want to make America proud again"; etc. Successful fund-raising campaigns have many times taken a similar tack: "It's a matter of life and breath"; "United Way— thanks to you, it's working"; "It hurts to go to bed hungry."

Clearly, well-conceptualized and well-communicated causes have enormous power to coalesce public opinion and to motivate people to act. The organization or institution for which you seek funds need not have a slick slogan, but it must have a believable cause—it must stand for something that people can perceive as important to them and to the things they cherish.

At least two factors make a cause believable: impact and immediacy:

○ *Impact:*   Your organization must have direct impact on the lives of those whom you intend to solicit. People must be inclined to say, when they hear about your aspirations, "Yes, it's *important* that we do that." Sometimes impact is mostly a matter of geography. If you're a turkey farmer who lives 600 miles from a big airport, you aren't likely to respond to an appeal from an association of turkey farmers for funds to fight noisy jet aircraft. But what if you and your turkeys are only 50 miles from a major airport?

○ *Immediacy:*   Your organization must be involved in work that merits attention *now, today, as soon as possible;* hence, "We want to cure cancer *in your lifetime.*" Without a strong sense of immediacy, you will have difficulty stirring prospects and volunteers to action.

A third factor, one easily overlooked, also deserves attention. It involves *you*—your attitude, commitment, outlook— the whole way in which you view the worth of your work. You cannot function with maximum effectiveness on behalf of a cause in which you do not fully believe and to which you yourself have not made a financial contribution. If you find yourself in that position, you should, as a matter of personal integrity, step aside and give your organization a chance to strengthen its leadership.

An important part of establishing the cause is the *case statement.* This is a written declaration telling what your organization does, what it has accomplished, what it intends to do in the future, and why it is worthy of people's financial support. Put the statement in *writing.* This is important for two reasons. First, it will help you to communicate with volunteers and prospects (you'll refer to it repeatedly in preparing news releases, proposals, brochures, letters, and speeches). And second, it will force you and your colleagues to give the matter the serious, thoughtful attention it deserves. Many case statements are too long (few people want to read 1,500 words all about *your* organization), too self-congratulatory, too inward-looking and provincial, too noncommittal. An example of a short but effective case statement used by the American Cancer Society is presented in Figure 3-1.

BUILDING THE ORGANIZATION

Chances are, whether you are an amateur or professional fund-raiser, your organization already exists—it doesn't have to be built. But even if that is the case, an understanding of the basics of fund-raising organization will make you a better fund-raiser. It will also prepare you to expand your organization when the time comes.

Line functions in a fund-raising organization (those that contribute *directly* to raising money) typically include: Planned (Deferred) Giving, Annual Giving, Institutional Giving (foundations and corporations), and Special Projects (individuals and "targets of opportunity"). Staff functions (those that contribute *indirectly* to raising money) typically include: Legal Counsel, Accounting and Financial Services, Research, Communications, and Data Processing/Records.

In a small fund-raising organization (one to three full-time people plus volunteers), line and staff functions are, of course, combined. For example, the individual in charge of Institutional Giving is his own researcher, communicator and accountant.

A fund-raising organization of medium size (four to nine full-time people plus volunteers) can usually afford the luxury of some separate staff functions. These should be those that require highly specialized skills, including Legal Counsel, Data Processing/Records and Communications.

A fund-raising organization of large size (10 or more people plus volunteers) typically has many line and staff functions, some of which are highly specialized. Some large universities, for example, have separate "asset disposition" departments that specialize in converting non-cash donations (land, automobiles, jewelry, collections, etc.) to cash by selling them.

Model organization charts for small, medium and large fund-raising organizations are shown in Figures 3-2, 3-3, and 3-4.

Whether your organization consists of only you and a volunteer or two, or you and 50 others, here is a checklist that ought to be reviewed periodically. Some of your answers may suggest the need to make changes.

☐ Are your duties and those of your associates about evenly divided?*

☐ Are your duties and those of your associates logically, functionally grouped?* For example, if you are handling Planned Giving, you should probably be handling Special Projects as well—both involve individual prospects and have many parallels.

☐ Are you making effective use of the many services available all around you? For example, if you are on a college campus, are you having the college's full-time public communications director write news releases, rather than you doing it? Are you spending time and money on image-building publications when those prepared by the college will serve just as well? Are you using student writing and art talent? (Don't overlook students as fund-raisers, either. On a growing number of campuses they are proving to be extremely effective. At Brigham Young University, for example, students raised $400,000 from other students, individuals, foundations and corporations for a new library addition.)

☐ Are you making effective use of volunteers? Some *will* perform, but only if they feel they are genuinely needed. Suggestion: Give them legitimate, challenging assignments in which the results and rewards are measurable and meaningful. Avoid, however, imposing heavily on their time.

☐ Are you involving your secretary in planning meetings and other activities so that she has the total organizational perspective? She can handle many time-consuming details if you'll keep her fully informed.

☐ Are you preparing and maintaining a yearly calendar with key events (dates direct mail pieces are to be sent out, for example) clearly announced? Without such a calendar, you cannot efficiently plan and manage your work and that of your associates.

---

* Not applicable to one-person organizations.

☐ Are you striving to grow professionally by reading current professional literature (principally magazines and newsletters), meeting and corresponding with other fund-raisers (seminars, conferences and conventions are excellent for this purpose), and affiliating with professional organizations?

☐ Are you involving professional fund-raising consultants in those inevitable instances when their services are indispensable?

☐ Are you evaluating your performance against some objective yardstick, including amount raised and operating expenses?

☐ Are you secure and mature enough to actively seek and accept honest criticism, and then to take the appropriate corrective action?

☐ Are you maintaining current, detailed job descriptions for each employee position?

☐ Are you establishing *written* policies for your organization's principal functions?

☐ Are you familiar with legislation (state and federal) affecting charitable solicitation, and are you in compliance?

☐ Are you doing everything possible to maximize the amount of time you and your associates devote to *asking* (assuming you are in line positions)?

If a fund-raising organization is involved in a capital campaign,* it is usually well advised to maintain its existing organization and augment it with volunteer and part-time help only as necessary. For example, the fund-raiser for a university in the Midwest met most of his staff needs for a centennial year capital campaign by using retired alumni. He asked a successful, retired industrialist to help call on corporate prospects; a retired attorney to help with planned giving pre-

---

* Arthur C. Frantzreb, fund-raising authority writing in *Fund Raising Management*, offers this helpful definition of a capital campaign:
". . . usually an all-out, total constituency, person-to-person solicitation for a series of specific objectives within a given time frame with pledges or statements of intent payable over three to five years."

sentations; and a retired physician, who had doctored the school's athletic teams for many years, to call on doctors and dentists. All served without pay.

A common practice in capital campaigns is to appoint an honorary campaign chairman and, sometimes, campaign committee. These are usually well-known, respected community, state or even national leaders. They impart prestige, impact and influence to the campaign. (You can usually find their names and titles in bold face type on all campaign literature!) Their main function, though, is to open doors.

Unquestionably, such individuals can be an asset. Make certain, however, that you clearly define and limit their powers and responsibilities. Make their involvement simple and easy. Tell them how long they are to serve. Don't give them a long list of assignments. Keep meetings to a minimum. Be content to use their names, influence and contacts—this is their principal value. Finally, make them answerable to the full-time director.

IDENTIFYING/EVALUATING PROSPECTS

Consider this: Ninety percent of the money in a typical fundraising campaign comes from 10 percent of the prospects, about 85 percent of whom are *individuals* (as opposed to foundations and corporations). This means that you must carefully identify, evaluate and file the names of *quality* individual* prospects.

Where do you find prospects? Try these sources:

○ *Past Donors:*   Thousands of years of cumulative fund-raising experience nationwide make it clear that past donors are almost always the best prospects for future gifts. If your records have been properly maintained, you should have a file full of information about these people, including date and amount of their last gift.
○ *Records of Your Organization:*   Categories vary, depending on the organization, but include: parents, employees, students, faculty, friends, vendors, visitors, patients, volunteers, awardees and individuals who in one way or another have expressed inter-

---

* Suggestions for identifying foundation and corporation prospects are given in Chapter 5.

est in your work (perhaps via a complimentary letter to you or others).

o *Donors to Other Charitable Organizations:*   Some people make it a practice to give to charity. Giving is part of their life style. Consequently, they are excellent prospects. Watch for their names in newspaper articles, "honor rolls of giving" published by other charities, on buildings and facilities in your community, etc. Some fund-raisers freely trade donor lists. This is an acceptable practice unless you have a special relationship with your donors that may preclude it. For example, a donor may have asked you to keep his contribution confidential. Obviously, giving his name to another fund-raiser would be improper. Also, bear in mind that when you trade names you may alienate some donors who didn't expressly forbid the practice, but who may feel you have "used" them.

o *Membership Rosters:*   These are excellent because they quickly enable you to identify people whose interests match those of your organization. For example, if you are trying to raise funds for a children's community orchestra in a city in Ohio, the membership lists of Ohio musical societies, clubs and associations are certain to be helpful.

o *Telephone Directory Yellow Pages:*   This one's so obvious, it's easy to overlook. Almost any fund-raising organization can find important prospects in the yellow-page listings under "A" alone, which typically includes Accountants, Architects and Associations.

At the risk of sounding too obvious, one of the best ways to find prospects is to start looking for them! Once you begin actively to look, *many* names will come to mind.

You can, of course, *buy* a list of people who logically could be expected to have some interest in your organization. This ought to be one of your last resorts. Bear in mind that if you can buy that list, everybody else can, too. Consequently, prospects supplied by commercial sources may well be up to their ears in fund-raising appeals from other charities.

Evaluating prospects is an extremely important function to which too many fund-raisers devote too little time. Prospect-evaluation usually attempts to answer three questions:

o How much can this individual give?
o Which aspect of our program is likely to interest him most?
o In what form is he most likely to make his gift (cash, securities, trust, bequest, etc.)?

Clues that will help you to answer these questions include the following:

QUESTION	CLUES
How much can this individual give?	*Profession/Occupation.* (Is he a church organist or an orthodontist?)
	Memberships. (Does he golf at Provo Public or Pebble Beach?)
	Hobbies. (Does he collect string or stringed instruments?)
	Possessions. (Does he live in a house or a mansion . . . drive a Beetle or a Bentley . . . own a plot or a section?)
Which aspect of our program is likely to interest him most?	*Source of Wealth.* (If he made it in oil, he *may* be interested in geology.)
	Special Problems. (If he has a retarded child, he *may* be interested in a school for exceptional children.)
	Need for Recognition. (If this looms large in his life, a building bearing his name *may* be the only answer.)
	Community Activities. (If he's a Scouter, he *may* be interested in buying a troop bus or building a troop lodge.)
	Past Giving Patterns. (If he's given to Cancer, Heart and Diabetes, he *may* also give to Cystic Fibrosis.)
In what form is he most likely to make his gift?	*Nature of His Holdings.* (If he has assets that have greatly appreciated in value since he bought them, he *may* wish to give them to you rather than sell them, thereby avoiding capital gains tax.)
	Income Requirements. (If he has substantial assets but cannot afford

to give up income from them, he
may wish to establish a charitable
annuity trust for himself and your
organization. This will probably
give him a fixed income for life. At
his death, the balance of the trust
assets will go to your organization.)
Tax Situation. (The possibilities
are almost endless here. Visit with
an attorney friend.)

One additional thought about how much to ask for: If
you're uncertain, try to err on the high side. Donors are almost *never* offended by being asked for too much (in fact,
they are usually flattered). And if you do ask for too much,
your donor can always suggest a smaller amount. On the
other hand, donors are frequently offended by being asked
for too little. A common reaction is, "So that's all they think
I'm worth!"

The mechanics of prospect-evaluation are best accomplished in a committee setting. Ideally, the committee should
consist of people with a large number of contacts—bankers,
attorneys, merchants, coaches, physicians, insurance salesmen, real estate brokers, CPA's, etc. If you pick the right people for your committee, they will give you many excellent insights. You may be able to call these people as volunteers,
and ask them to meet with you monthly or bi-monthly. Large
fund-raising organizations typically have a standing "prospect-evaluation committee" chaired by full-time staff members.

A Prospect Identification/Evaluation Card is a helpful, almost indispensable tool in this whole process. A model card
is shown in Figure 3-5.

CULTIVATING PROSPECTS

Prospects, like peach trees, almost never produce to their
potential unless they are carefully cultivated. It is a demanding, sometimes difficult process, but a rewarding one.
Fund-raisers define cultivation in several ways, but let us
say here that cultivation is the sum total of activities that

convince a prospect that a given charity is worthy of his financial support and that lead him, ultimately, to make a contribution.

Cultivation is primarily an educational process accomplished, ideally, with a consummate sense of salesmanship. In the case of small gifts, prospects may be cultivated at the same time they are asked. Door-to-door solicitation is a case in point. It usually involves a friendly, neighborly greeting, the exchange of some amenities, the projection of a pleasing personality, and *then* a request for a contribution. Well-executed direct mail pieces work much the same way. It's best, of course, if the prospect has *some* background about the organization—perhaps via a news story published in a local paper—but it isn't imperative. People have been known to give—$5, $10—without it.

If, however, you hope to attract large gifts from individuals,* substantial advanced planning and months, even years of cultivation activities are often necessary. Some prospects will not give until they are virtually positive that a given charity is a sound philanthropic investment. This knowledge can only be secured in a long-term relationship.

It might be well to say what cultivation is *not*. It is not a series of extravagant, pre-giving "bribes" (dinners, favors, gifts, trips, deals) designed to make the prospect feel obligated. It is not a shopping list of commitments that come due when the gift comes in. It is not, in fact, an agreement to deliver on promises of any kind other than those that naturally and properly accompany charitable giving. Be extremely wary of any prospect who makes demands and for whom charitable intent seems to be a distant, idealistic notion. Contributions from such individuals are almost never worthwhile, and a satisfactory relationship with them is seldom possible.

The following "cultivation canons" have proven to be realistic, functional and effective:

○ Earn your prospect's friendship. Take a sincere interest in him. Get to know him and appreciate him.

---

* This section deals exclusively with cultivating *individuals*. Foundations and corporations are not *cultivated* in the true meaning of the word. Nevertheless, some of what is presented here is appropriate for some foundation and corporation prospects.

○ Be prepared to give as well as to receive.
○ Help your prospect to understand that if he contributes to your organization, he will benefit by becoming a more fulfilled, complete, happier human being. In the final analysis, giving is an ennobling, spiritual experience. Help your prospect come to this realization.
○ Convince your prospect in a quiet way—through actions more than words—that the objectives of your organization are worthy of his support, and that they translate into practical, measurable results—a better school, bigger hospital, cleaner community, healthier world, etc.
○ Demonstrate to your prospect that you and your associates believe in what you are doing—that you are committed, competent, and, again, worthy of his support.
○ Make your organization meaningful to your prospect in his frame of reference, on his scale of values. If, for example, you are seeking funds for a hospital and geriatrics is your prospect's special interest, talk about geriatrics—not about your shiny-new maternity ward.

Specifically, what steps are involved in cultivation?

Let's assume that you are in charge of fund-raising for a small, private college. The college operates a special school for learning-disabled children. One of your priority projects is to raise $3,500 to buy visual aids for the school. Items needed include slide and motion picture projectors, hearing aid devices, and a library of films, pictures and demonstration models.

You have identified a Mr. Hillman as a top prospect to contribute the $3,500. He is a successful, retired automobile dealer in your town who has been active in community affairs. He once headed up a local Heart Fund drive. How do you cultivate him? The following is a suggested course of action (it must, of course, be adjusted as individual circumstances warrant):

○ Take a sincere interest in Mr. Hillman. Find out more about him —number of children, hobbies, schedule, health, accomplishments, close friends, birth place, education, religious and political persuasions, etc.
○ Put him on the college's mailing list for materials that should interest him: newsletter published by the School of Business, calendar of upcoming events, evening school class schedule, etc.

o Send him an article about the school for learning-disabled children, and include a brief, "thought you would be interested" cover letter from the college president.

o Have the president call him a week or so later and invite him to the campus for lunch. The president should offer to pick him up at his home. (A mutual friend of both Mr. Hillman and the president would be helpful here. He could extend the invitation to Mr. Hillman at the president's request, and attend the luncheon himself to make introductions and facilitate conversation.)

o At the luncheon, talk in a low-key way about the college's accomplishments and needs. *Listen* to what Mr. Hillman has to say, and try to "read" his reactions.

o After lunch, take Mr. Hillman on a tour of the campus, including the school for learning-disabled children. Let him talk with the teachers and meet the students. In an easy, careful way mention the important work of the school and the progress the students are making. Again, "read" his reactions.

o About a week after Mr. Hillman's visit, have the president send him a letter in the vein of "it was nice to have you here."

o Continue to send Mr. Hillman materials of interest. (You should have some fresh insights as a result of his visit.)

o Invite him to be the president's guest at a campus activity you believe he would enjoy (play, sports events, lecture, exhibit, etc.).

o Sincerely seek his advice and counsel on matters about which he is qualified to speak. You could, for example, invite him to speak to a business class about how to operate a successful automobile dealership.

o If the signals have been neutral or positive to this point, make an appointment with him to ask for the $3,500.

Obviously, cultivation is never this cut and dried. You will encounter mixed responses and disappointments along the way. Mr. Hillman's health may not permit him to visit the campus. He may feel uncomfortable with young people. He may be an inept speaker. There are many different possibilities.

It is important—even essential—for Mr. Hillman to sense that you plan to ask for the contribution before you actually do so. This is a necessary, desirable part of cultivation. Some fund-raisers nurture the notion that they can ambush prospects. This is a sure-fire way to fail.

Once Mr. Hillman senses that you plan to ask for a contribution, you will probably get one of three signals: (1) "No, I'm not interested" (this can be communicated in a variety of ways, but often takes the form of a refusal to see you); (2) "Yes, I'm interested" (he may well take the initiative in talking about a contribution) or (3) silence—that is, neither a "yes" or "no" (this may be interpreted as a positive sign, since the prospect may well be saying to himself, "I'm willing to listen to what he has to say").

If the signal is negative, you should, in a way, be grateful. Mr. Hillman is making it easy for you—and freeing you to move to the next name on your list.

Maybe we'll cure cancer without your help, but don't bet your life on it.

The way it stands today, one American out of four will someday have cancer. That means it will strike some member in two out of three American families.

To change those statistics we have to bring the promise of research to everyday reality. And to expand our detection program and techniques. And that takes money. Lots of money. Money we won't have—unless you help us.

The American Cancer Society will never give up the fight. Maybe we'll find the answers even without your help. But don't bet your life on it.

American Cancer Society
We want to cure cancer in your lifetime.

Figure 3-1.   Model Case Statement

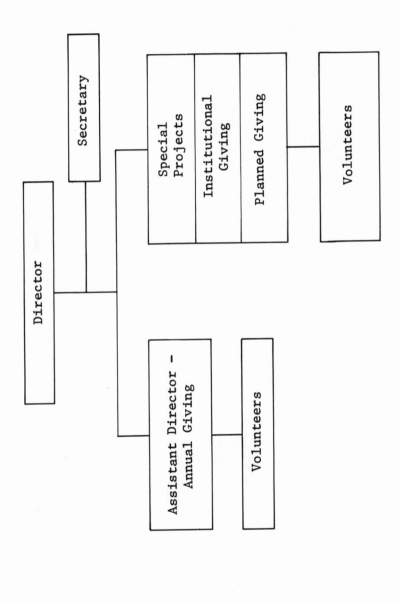

Figure 3-2. Organization Chart for Small Fund-raising Operation

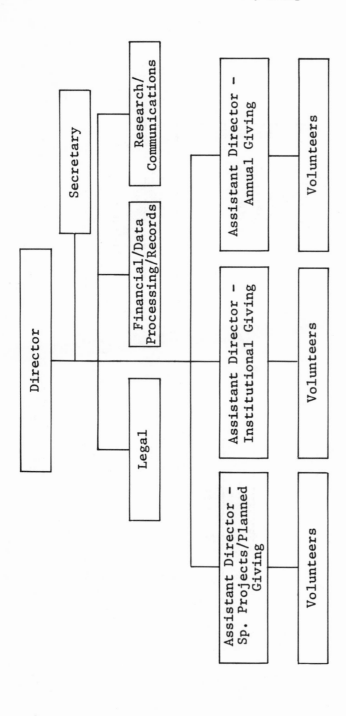

Figure 3-3.   Organization Chart for Medium-Sized Fund-raising Operation

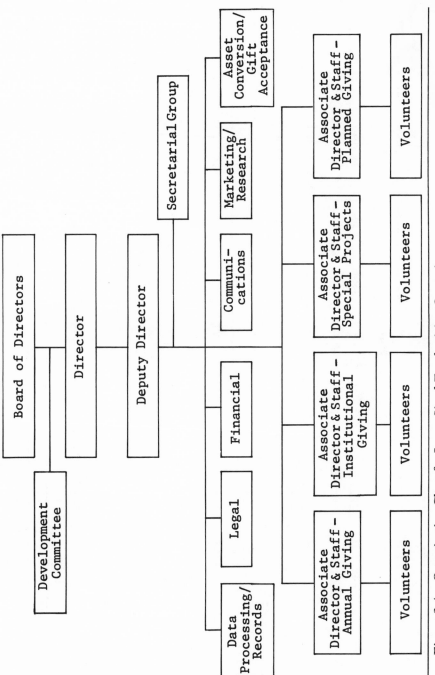

Figure 3-4.   Organization Chart for Large-Sized Fund-raising Operation

```
PROSPECT IDENTIFICATION/EVALUATION CARD  Name_____

Address_____  City_____  State___  Zip___  Phone (  )___

Age___  Occupation_____  Health Condition_____  Religion_____

Marital Status:  ( )Married   ( )Single   ( )Widow(er)   ( )Divorced

Spouse's Name and Age_____   Condition of Spouse's Health_____

Children's Names and Ages_____

Prospect's Memberships (Rotary, etc.)_____

Prospect's Honors, Recognition, etc._____

Aprox. Annual Income $_____  Est. Net Worth $_____  Political Pref.___

List Assets (securities, real estate, etc.)_____

Is any of this property highly appreciated?  If so, specify_____

Has prospect given to other charities?  If so, which ones/how much?_____

                    Prospect's Attorney/Accountant_____

Prospect's Interests and Hobbies_____

Special Qualities, Needs, Problems Relating to Prospect_____
```

Figure 3-5.   Prospect Identification/Evaluation Card

Chapter Four

ASKING TECHNIQUES AND TOOLS

This chapter introduces, explains and evaluates the four basic asking techniques and the communication tools associated with them. Application of the techniques and tools to actual asking situations receives special, independent attention in the next chapter.

IN-PERSON TECHNIQUE

In-person asking consistently produces more and larger contributions than any other solicitation technique. Unfortunately, some fund-raisers avoid it simply because they lack the confidence to look a prospect in the eye and ask. They prefer to ask *in abstentia,* usually by means of a letter or brochure. Result: They develop few new contacts, miss out on opportunities to speak personally for their cause and raise far less money than they otherwise would. Granted, in-person asking is not the most comfortable way to ask. It does, however, get easier with practice. Moreover, once you master it, you have access to rewards available in no other way.

The fund-raiser who makes his appeal face-to-face with his

51

prospect has three major advantages: (1) *Urgency and Commitment.* His personal presence tells the prospect that the matter at hand is an important one to which the fund-raiser is clearly, sincerely committed. It also tells the prospect that the fund-raiser regards him as someone worthy of personal attention. These factors make for a positive beginning—before a word is spoken. (2) *Optimum, Responsive Communication.* Face-to-face asking gives the fund-raiser the enormous advantage of asking with his total being—voice, eyes, mannerisms—and all that they mean in terms of conviction, sincerity, charm and persuasiveness. Such a fund-raiser has the advantage of receiving feedback from the prospect so that he can tailor his presentation for maximum impact. (3) *Pressure.* It's hard to say "no" to another human being whose cause is just, who has appealed to your noblest instincts, and who is only three feet away. Some of us can be ogres when it comes to turning down an appeal by mail, over TV, or even on the telephone. But the person who asks us face to face is a force to be reckoned with!

If you have a small prospect market or a large volunteer force, you may be able to ask all of your prospects in person—an ideal situation. The pastor of a small congregation, for example, could probably manage a personal appeal to each parishioner. Many fund-raisers find, however, that they must limit in-person asking to those most likely to give the largest gifts. Big universities, as a case in point, may have as many as 200,000 alumni. Obviously, only a fraction of these can be asked in person.

Good fund-raising etiquette demands that individual prospects (as opposed to foundations and corporations) be asked in person when (a) you are asking for a large gift—one of several thousand dollars or more, or (b) your prospect is a distinguished individual who deserves your personal attention, particularly if he is conveniently available to you. It would clearly be bad form, for example, to send a solicitation letter to a prominent local physician asking him for a $5,000 contribution. That appeal should be made in person.

The communication tools appropriate for use with the in-person asking technique range from nothing more than the fund-raiser's voice and sense of salesmanship to elaborate, custom-designed slide presentations and written requests. Remember, however, that the very fact that you take the time and make the effort to prepare materials of *some* kind is likely to favorably impress your prospect. He may well say to himself, "This fellow has done his homework—must be serious about this thing."

Suggested in-person asking tools and guidelines for their use are presented in the paragraphs that follow.

Charts

These can enhance almost any in-person presentation. They help to focus attention and to move speaker and listener from point to point in a logical, orderly fashion. Use type of 18 points or larger, and limit your text to key words. If you don't have access to a good sign painter or free-hand letterer, type the charts on an IBM Selectric in a clean, bold, sans serif face in the largest size available (the Orator face is excellent), then have a printer enlarge them photographically. You get a bonus with this approach—the unenlarged typewritten sheets which you can give the prospect as a handout. They will serve as an excellent summary of the entire presentation.

Charts and other visual aids (photographs, maps, diagrams, tables, illustrations) are especially helpful if you are asking for money for a complex or technical subject. Take care, however, that visual aids do not dominate the presentation. Concentrate on the prospect, not on the aids.

A graphically effective chart that makes good use of key words is shown in Figure 4-1.

Written Requests

Sometimes called "proposals," these are prepared in many different formats, and their content varies widely. Almost all, however, share a common purpose: to help sell projects to prospects.

For in-person asking, the written request is properly used after the presentation, as a reinforcement device and decision-making document. If, for example, you are asking for a large gift—$10,000 or more—or if the project is an involved one that requires the study of several people (including attorneys, family members and financial advisers), you are not likely to get an answer in the meeting. Also, if you are asking for a corporate or foundation gift, you may have to wait for the decision of a board of directors or some other governing body. It is under these circumstances that the written request is most useful.

If the prospect responds favorably during the presentation, you might be well advised to keep the written request in your briefcase. Why? There is safety in generalities: Written detail, which is subject to being shown to others, may diminish rather than enhance your project's appeal to the donor and his advisers.

Some fund-raisers go to substantial expense to prepare plush, full-color written requests. *Don't do it!* Most prospects look for substance, not ornamentation. You can produce attractive, functional, economical written requests by printing a year's supply of page layout sheets in one color, and then printing the text for individual requests, as they come along, in black ink on the layout sheets. Stick to standard page size (8½″ × 11″), and use an economical binding system that allows for changing pages, such as Sure-Lox (General Binding Corporation). Two different styles of layout sheets, with text imprinted, are shown in Figures 4-2 and 4-3.

There is an ongoing, spirited discussion among fund-raisers as to the ideal length of a written request. Some say it should not exceed one or two pages. Others argue convincingly for at least 10 pages, sometimes backed by appendices.

The "two-track" approach is a good solution. The first "track"—a one-page summary up front—answers the argument of those who say all the prospect really needs—and reads—is a quick, clear overview. The second "track"—a 10- or 12-page in-depth treatment of the project—answers the argument of those who say that you only have one "shot" at the prospect, so you must tell your whole story.

The major sections for a model two-track written request are presented and described in the paragraphs that follow.

COVER
Keep it simple, functional, in good taste. Figure 4-4 shows a well designed solid-front request cover. You may, however,

prefer a window cover that displays the title (from the title page), thus making it possible to identify the request quickly by name.

TITLE PAGE
Include title of project, date prepared and name of submitting organization. Give careful thought to the title. It should set the tone and scope of the project, and make some kind of promise to the reader. Here are two good examples: (1) "The J. John Doe Food and Fiber Institute: Discovering and Implementing Practical Solutions to Immediate Problems—A Request for Funding Support," and (2) "Request for Funds for a New Lodge at Apple Dell Girls' Camp: An Important Investment in Our Community's Future."

A model title page is shown in Figure 4-5.

SUMMARY
In one page, introduce the project (including why it is important and what it will accomplish), ask for the money (if you will accept partial funding support, so state), tell how and when the work will be accomplished, and give the qualifications of your organization to do the work.

An effective one-page summary is shown in Figure 4-6.

THE NEED
Tell why the project is needed. Give just enough detail to establish credibility. Tone is important here. Don't talk about problems. Talk, rather, about opportunities. Help the prospect to see how he and your organization, working together, can make a contribution to society.

Opening paragraphs from a well-written "Need" section are presented in Figure 4-7.

MEETING THE NEED
Unveil your plan for accomplishing the proposed project. Radiate confidence and enthusiasm. This is your chance to impress the prospect with your vision and ability to plan, organize, and manage. If you have already, on your own, taken steps to help meet the need, say so. In California, for example, a group of parents was seeking funds for playground equipment. They pointed out to prospects that they had

spent the last six Saturdays preparing the site. Duly impressed, their prospects gave.

"Meeting the Need" should answer at least the following questions:

○ When will the project begin, what are its key mileposts, and when will it end?
○ What tasks are involved and how will they be accomplished?
○ How will the project be organized, where will it be conducted, and who will direct it?
○ Who will have overall project responsibility, and who will disburse the funds?

EXPECTED RESULTS

Tell what you expect will happen if the project is funded and carried through to completion. Take pains not to promise too much. Most donors don't expect their contributions to reform the world. They are satisfied if what they give helps even a small group of people in a meaningful way.

BUDGET

Provide a detailed tabulation of projected income and expenditures. Be sure to include financial support provided by your organization, even if it's in the form of personnel, facilities, equipment, supplies, etc. This is important, because it is to your advantage to tell your prospects that you believe enough in the project to commit your own resources to it. Above all, make your budget *realistic*. If you pad it or if you are too conservative, you will lose credibility in the eyes of your prospect (foundations are especially perceptive about budgets). If your project is funded and the budget is unrealistic, ultimately both the project and your relationship with the donor will suffer.

A model budget is shown in Figure 4-8.

RELATED EXPERIENCE (OPTIONAL)

If your organization is particularly well qualified for the project because of extensive related experience and success with similar projects, this is the place to speak out. For example, a small college seeking travel funds for its debate team proudly—and properly—told prospects about its string of three regional debate championships.

PERSONNEL (OPTIONAL)

Ordinarily, personnel can be covered in "Meeting the Need." If, however, your project involves several people in key positions, you may want to present their resumés in this separate section. Even if you take this approach, keep the resumés short and to the point. This is not the time or place for ego trips.

Short but informative resumés are shown in Figure 4-9.

WHAT OTHERS SAY (OPTIONAL)

Sometimes it's more comfortable—and credible—to have others speak for you. This section enables you to do that. It consists of statements in support of your organization or project. Get the permission of each individual to use his statement, then put his name and title with it. Avoid crediting statements to faceless people, such as "community leader" or "food franchise executive."

ORGANIZATION IN BRIEF (OPTIONAL)

This is a one-page, in-a-nutshell listing of the principal features of your organization. It's a convenient, readable way to handle important but basic information.

A model "in brief" listing is shown in Figure 4-10.

Slide-Sound Shows

You have two choices here: (1) Put together a show specifically for the project at hand, or (2) Use an existing, off-the-shelf show that deals with your organization in general terms.

Custom-made, professionally produced slide-sound shows are expensive (as much as $5,000 for a 12-minute production). Consequently, they can be justified only if you have a large dollar goal (say $75,000 or more), and you expect to present them to several "blue chip" prospects. They can, however, be extremely effective: The combination of strong, full-color images, music, sound effects, and skillful narration can get at the very circuitry of human emotion.

It's possible, of course, for you to produce your own show. If you are inexperienced at it, you might begin with Eastman Kodak's excellent publication, *Planning and Producing Slide*

Programs, then visit with a scriptwriter, photographer and sound man.

A large university produced a custom-made slide-sound show not only for a particular project, but for a particular prospect. It involved a major campus complex to be named after the prospect, and included mockups of the buildings displaying the prospect's name. It paid off—to the tune of $4 million.

Off-the-shelf shows will help to introduce an organization, set tone, communicate values and give background. They can be worthwhile, especially if your prospect is not familiar with your organization. Resist the temptation to use a dated show —one over three or four years old. You won't get away with it (fashions, makeup, and hair style change too fast), and you'll come off looking—well, tacky.

If you use a slide-sound show, custom-made or off-the-shelf, make certain that it does not dominate the presentation. Allow ample time for friendly, personalized give and take—and for asking. *Never* have the show or any other tool do the asking in the in-person technique. Asking is *your* job. Otherwise, you might as well use another, less demanding solicitation technique, such as direct mail.

Unless you have access to truly professional help, avoid exotic, multiple-screen, multiple-projector shows. They are difficult, demanding and unnecessary.

Brochures, Folders, Special Print Media

Use these to add color, excitement, and graphic impact to your presentation. Do not use them in place of the written request described earlier. Why? Because fund-raising projects inevitably change from conceptualization to completion— change in size, purpose, personnel, location and even dollar amount. If you use the written request in the format described, you can easily, economically update your information. Brochures, folders, and special print media, on the other hand, cannot be economically updated. Invariably, fund–raisers who prepare such pieces as their primary asking documents at the outset of a campaign end up reprinting them before the campaign is complete.

Of all the communication tools for in-person asking, these pieces of literature are the least important. They are nice, but not really necessary. Often their principal value is internal—they force decision makers to commit themselves in writing to policies, procedures, objectives, schedules, etc. If you do decided to prepare them, here are some time-tested guidelines:

○ Focus on a single, simple message and get it into the title. Some good examples: "Hospitals Are for Helping" (for a community-wide hospital expansion campaign); "Paths to Progress for American Indians" (for a university project to attract foundation funds for American Indian programs); "Time to Make a Choice" (for a campaign encouraging businessmen to contribute to a conservative, "free enterprise" college).

○ Avoid "label" titles such as these: "Jonesville Community Church Fund," "Sixth Annual Alumni Campaign," "1977 Hillsdale Boys' Club Drive." Don't exactly put you on the edge of your seat, do they?

○ Use words that lend themselves to strong graphic design treatment. For example, the above-listed "Paths to Progress" piece featured a series of lines (paths) disappearing into the distance under the title.

○ Try, where practical, to include the magic word "you" or variations of it in the title. Some examples: "You and the Future of Flint Little League," "What You Should Know About Giving to the Church," "Why You're the Most Important Part of Dixon PTA."

○ Keep copy brief, direct, to the point. Use tabulations and listings to break up type and facilitate easy reading.

○ Emphasize *people* and how they will benefit from what you are doing.

○ Avoid extremes in color, typography and size. If, for example, you make a brochure 3¾" × 8½", it will easily fit into a #10 envelope, and you can use it as a mail-answering piece or in other kinds of correspondence.

○ Include a coupon to encourage prospect response. A model coupon is shown in Figure 4-11.

○ Hire a good graphic designer. If the piece is worth doing at all, it's worth professional design. Fees vary, of course, but plan on $100 minimum.

Pledge Card

If your prospect answers "yes" during the meeting, but is not prepared to write you a check for the full amount, *have him fill out a pledge card.* (See Figure 4-12.) This document is invaluable, because it helps you to:

○ Commit the prospect to make the gift.
○ Set the amount to be contributed.
○ Establish whether the gift is to be restricted to a particular project or used for general purposes.
○ Set a payment schedule.

Even if the gift is to be given in deferred form, such as an annuity trust, the pledge card is still useful, simply because it formalizes the prospect's promise to give.

You should carefully file and maintain completed pledge cards, so that they are available for followup purposes. Note that the card shown in Figure 4-12 is IBM card size, so that it fits into a standard file.

GROUP TECHNIQUE

Under the right circumstances, this approach is next in effectiveness to in-person asking. Its great strength is social and peer pressure.

Let's look at the group technique in action. In an Illinois city of 50,000, a respected business leader held a dinner for 25 of the city's most successful businessmen. In his formal, written invitations to them, he said he wanted to discuss "a matter of importance to the city's future." He greeted them at the door, and, after they had eaten, he stood up and said something like this:

"Gentlemen, I want you to know that I appreciate your attendance here this evening. You know that there's no such thing as a free lunch—or dinner! I think you know, too, that our city swimming pool needs to be repaired and enlarged. In its present condition, it's unsafe for our children. The city doesn't have the tax revenues to do the job—and won't have for several years. I know *we* have the means—and I believe *we* have the desire—to do something about it. I will contribute a dollar for every dollar each of you contributes. You must, however, contribute a minimum of $500. What do you say?"

This bold, talented and selfless fund-raiser had arranged for two of the businessmen in attendance to lead off by pledging gifts of $1,000 each. Predictably, the others followed suit. Pledge cards were completed by every businessman before the evening ended.

Too much pressure, you say? Perhaps. Clearly, in some circumstances, a lower-key approach would be safer and more appropriate. You could, for example, hold a luncheon or dinner, explain your project and the benefits it will offer your community, pass out pledge cards and *invite* those in attendance to contribute. If you perform well, a few will pledge then and there, and a few others will mail in their cards to you. Some, of course, will not respond. You should solicit these in-person or by telephone.

The group technique is most likely to succeed when three conditions exist: (1) The person who asks is respected, influential and agreeably aggressive; (2) the group is united by religion, politics, profession, national origin or some other strong element of commonality,* and (3) the project or cause is one in which the group deeply believes.

The communication tools appropriate for the group technique, in addition to the pledge card, include all of those recommended for the in-person technique.

TELEPHONE

The telephone is the third most effective solicitation technique. It is best used in intensive, one- or two-night calling campaigns known variously as "telefunds," "telethons," and "fonathons." Unquestionably, these campaigns enable you to reach large numbers of people economically and with reason-

---

* Sometimes the strong motivating force is adversity. For example, the parents and wives of American servicemen missing in action or unaccounted for in Vietnam gave freely of their own funds—and were effective in raising funds from others—in support of their search for their loved ones.

ably good impact. In addition, they minimize the time and effort required of volunteer workers—an important consideration for many organizations.

If you have only a few people to call, you can, of course,
ask by telephone without organizing a calling campaign. But
if you have only a few prospects to ask, and if they are available locally, you might as well use the in-person technique.
It will increase your chances of success.

Contributions given in response to telephone solicitation
are not large. Many institutions find that they average between $20 and $40 per donor. In most cases, the average must
be at least $10 to justify the time and effort involved. It is, of
course, inappropriate to ask for large sums of money by telephone. One possible exception: special campaigns featuring
celebrity volunteers who call "blue chip" prospects.

Conducting a telefund—the term preferred herein—is not
difficult. It does, however, require substantial organization,
detail work and followup. Here are the steps:

○ Compile a calling list. Research the names, addresses and telephone numbers of people who could reasonably be expected to
contribute to your cause. In the case of educational institutions,
alumni and parents of students are ideal prospects. Design and
print telefund cards (Figure 4-13), and enter on them the information from your list. (The card shown in Figure 4-13 is a basic
one. Institutions with years of telefund experience use sophisticated cards with computer-printed entries. Some even list past
giving records; year the prospect graduated from the institution
if applicable; name of spouse; and whether or not the prospect
works for a matching gift company.) Note that the card shown in
Figure 4-13 consists of two parts. The top part is a "pledge re-
minder/thank you" that the volunteer fills in and signs if the
prospect pledges. It is designed so that the address will show
through a window envelope, and it is mailed to the pledgee. The
bottom part is a "record of call" that the volunteer fills in, and
the organization retains.

○ Recruit one volunteer caller for every 40 prospects you want to
contact in a single evening of calling. Get more than you need,
because you will probably have some last-minute dropouts. Recruit from among those who are friends of your cause—past givers, loyal alumni, former officers, etc. If you have a choice, opt
for salesmen, professionals and people with good speaking skills.
Recruit them in person or by telephone.

○ Locate a facility with a large number of telephones, and reserve it for one evening. Banks and stock brokerage firms are excellent. Many will make their facilities available free of charge as a good-will gesture. Avoid Fridays, weekends and holidays.

○ Two weeks before the telefund, call the volunteers and give them a date and place. Ask them to be there at 6 P.M. sharp. Tell them you will serve a box lunch or some kind of "packaged" dinner (something self-contained with napkins, plastic utensils, etc.). Ask them to plan to stay until 9:30 P.M.

○ Five days before the telefund, send the volunteers a friendly post card reminding them of the telefund date, place and time.

○ Two nights before the telefund, call the volunteers and confirm their plans to attend. Dropouts will surface now; you should have allowed for them.

○ Arrive at the facility a half-hour early. Tape a "welcome" sign to the front door. Make sure everything is in order. Put the telefund cards and dinner by each phone. Set up any visual aids you intend to use.

○ Greet the volunteers warmly at the door. To help with names and introductions, you may wish to have them fill out identification cards and pin them on.

○ When all the volunteers have arrived, greet them as a group, thank them for coming and invite them to begin eating.

○ When they are nearly finished eating (about 6:30), begin your orientation. Put them at ease by being relaxed, almost casual (they need this, especially if it's their first experience with telephone solicitation). Tell them how much you hope to raise during the evening. They should already be converted to your cause, but touch briefly on it. Sample: "What you do this evening can make a real difference—a lasting difference—in the quality of education available to Central College students." Introduce them to the telefund card, and tell them how to fill it out. (Some telefund directors use a large blowup of the card for this purpose. Others provide a handout giving step-by-step instructions. A few institutions use slide shows or filmstrips.) Ask them to group the telefund cards into piles, depending on the results of each call: one pile for "not home," another for "pledged," another for "wrong number," etc. (See bottom part of card, Figure 4-13.)

○ Review the elements of a good telephone approach. Tell them to relax, be themselves, and speak naturally. Read a model approach to them—something like this:

"Hello, Pat Johnson? (Response.) "This is Kelly Walker calling. I understand that you graduated from Central College in

1969 . . . is that right?" (Response.) "I'm calling with a group of telefund volunteers, and we need your help. We're raising money to enable Central to continue its great work. Right now, the fieldhouse expansion is a special need. Can we count on you for a contribution . . . say $25?* (Response. If it's positive, thank the individual, confirm her/his address, and hang up. If it's negative, then proceed as follows.) "I can certainly understand how you feel—things are tight for many of us these days. We're not really looking for a large contribution. If it would be easier, perhaps you could pay some now and the balance later. What do you think?" (Response. Quite often, the individual will say something like, "Well . . . maybe I could give you half now and half in a couple of months." Your response might then be, "That's great, Pat. We appreciate your generosity." You then confirm the address. If, however, the prospect still resists, it's best to back off. Try to end on a positive note: "It's been nice talking with you, Pat. Perhaps you can help us another time. Have a good evening.")

o Ask if there are any questions, then tell them to begin calling (it should be about 6:50 by now). It's good strategy to arrange the cards so that the inexperienced volunteers will call the most promising prospects first—individuals who have given in the past or who you know are favorable to your program. Positive responses at the outset will boost confidence.
o Some fund-raisers use cowbells or other noisemakers to build volunteer espirit. Volunteers actuate them every time they receive a pledge. They help!
o Circulate among the volunteers to see how they are doing. Offer suggestions, give encouragement and be available to answer questions.
o Try to keep a running total of pledges received. Post the total periodically for all to see.
o At the end of the evening (about 9:15), announce the grand total, collect the cards and warmly thank each volunteer.
o Ask each volunteer to sign a "Thanks for the use of your desk" card or table tent (Figure 4-14), and leave it on the desk he used. Also, send a thank-you letter within a few days to the individual who let you use the facility. These are little things, but they can

---

*It's important to suggest a specific amount, or at least a giving range. Most prospects hesitate to make a specific pledge until they know the amount you have in mind.

make the difference between a "yes" and a "no" next time you want to use the facility.

o Mail the pledge reminder slips that very evening, or, the next day at the latest. Include a self-addressed remittance envelope.

o Send an upbeat reminder letter to those who have not sent in their contribution after a month. (A suggested letter is shown in Figure 4-15.) Institutions with sophisticated telefund programs use a reminder form with computer-printed entries. This is not necessarily more effective, just more efficient.) You may wish to take a softer reminder approach than that shown in Figure 4-15. You could, for example, begin your letter by thanking the individual for his pledge and giving a progress report on the campaign. You would then conclude by encouraging the pledgee to send in his contribution. If the pledgees don't respond to your letter, whatever approach you take, write them off. Further effort is probably not justified. If 60 percent or more of those who pledged pay, you've done well.

Some fund-raisers effectively combine direct mail with telefunds. The approach is to send a letter three weeks before the telefund to everyone on the calling list. The letter introduces the organization, explains the need for contributions and how they will be used, announces that the individual will be called and concludes with a P.S. like this: "In the event we are unable to reach you by telephone, a remittance envelope is enclosed for your convenience." There are three vital advantages to this approach: (1) It prepares prospects for your call and gives them helpful advance information (some people *never* give to a charity until they check it out); (2) it reduces the number of people your volunteers have to call, because some will give in direct response to the mailer, and (3) it ensures that you will reach virtually everyone on your calling list—if not by phone, then by mail.

Here is a quick look at three successful, real-life telefund campaigns that may help you get started:

o Directors of a center for retarded children were seeking funds for new recreational equipment. They conducted a telefund at the center and had parents of the children make the calls. The telefund was preceded by a TV interview with the directors over a local station. Amount raised: $1,175.

○ A college athletic director wanted to raise additional funds for athletic recruiting. He asked coaches and star players to call season ticket holders and alumni who had been athletes (this involved some long-distance). Amount raised: $4,800.

○ The adviser to a high school band needed travel funds for a trip to the Tournament of Roses Parade. Three hours before the telefund, the band appeared in a promotional parade with signs reading, "You'll Be Hearing More From Us Tonight!" Parents of the band members and teachers made the calls. Amount raised: $1,400.

DIRECT MAIL

Consult 10 different experts about how best to succeed with direct mail and you're likely to receive 10 distinctly different sets of instructions. The experts do agree on one thing, however: Direct mail is the least effective fund-raising solicitation technique. In fact, if five percent of the prospects you solicit by direct mail respond with a contribution, you're doing exceptionally well.

None of this means, however, that direct mail is not worth your while. For all of its shortcomings, direct mail accounted for a big chunk of the $29.4 billion American charities raised in 1976! The explanation? There is strength in numbers. Direct mail reaches millions of people with billions of messages. And increasingly those messages are not wild shots in the dark, but meticulously aimed appeals that hit their targets with sharpshooter accuracy.

The intent of this section is not to make you an expert in direct mail (that would require a separate volume), but to show you how to get started, and to offer some practical guidelines.

Address Lists

Whether a direct mailer succeeds or fails is determined principally by the quality of its address list. If, for example, the list contains the names and addresses of people who are sympathetic to your cause because of what they believe about

God or where they went to school, your mailer will probably succeed. If, on the other hand, your list is a haphazard collection of names mixed with high hopes, your mailer will probably not pay for itself.

You can rent address lists of the names of people who could reasonably be expected to contribute to your cause (list rental is, in fact, big business in the United States). If, for example, you are seeking funds to establish a premedical scholarship program, you might want to rent a "doctors and dentists" list. Several firms offer them, including one that has a 500,000-name list broken down by medical specialty. The cost varies, but plan on at least $30 per thousand names. The *Direct Mail List—Rates and Data*, a semi-annual publication of Standard Rate & Data Service, Inc., is the place to start. This directory, available at many libraries, references thousands of lists available for rent. In addition, the publisher issues updating bulletins throughout the year.

If you are just getting started in direct mail, you may be better off compiling your own address list. This is especially appropriate if you intend to solicit prospects who are uniquely identified with your organizaiton. For example, who is in a better position to prepare a list of alumni prospects than the fund-raising director of the college from which they graduated?

The following are rich sources of names for do-it-yourself lists:

○ *Past Donors.* These are your best prospects, of course, because they have already demonstrated their loyalty. Don't make the mistake, however, of soliciting potential "large gift" donors year after year by mail. They should be asked in person.
○ *People You Have Served.* Think of the people your organization has helped in some way—educated, counseled, operated on, toured with—they are ideal direct mail prospects.
○ *People You Will Serve in the Future.* Community college fund-raisers would do well to list the names of parents of local high school seniors; hospital fund-raisers, the names of heads of middle- and upper-income households in the community.
○ *People Who Share Your Interests.* Two examples: (1) The director of a drug-counseling center in need of funds listed local doctors, psychologists, counselors, social workers and judges. (2)

A Little League coach who needed funds for baseball equipment listed local high school and college coaches plus the players and owners of his city's professional baseball team.

The Mailer

If you've looked in your mail box lately, you know direct mailers come in all sizes, colors and styles. Basically, however, they are of two kinds: self-mailers and envelope mailers.

A self-mailer is a folder, brochure, flyer or other print–media piece sent without an envelope. The address is stamped or stuck to the mailer proper. These are popular with many fund-raisers because of their low cost. They are economical to print, process and mail. As a rule, however, they are less effective than envelope mailers. Unless they are well designed, they are not likely to command the attention given to a well-executed envelope mailer. Their most serious drawback, however, is that you cannot easily include a remittance envelope with them. (It *can* be done. You can, for example, staple or glue the remittance envelope inside. Also, you can order self-mailers from speciality printers with ingenious tear-off envelopes. But these solutions reduce or eliminate the self-mailer's low cost advantage.)

If you use a self-mailer, make it large enough to attract attention and to be inviting, and be sure to include a convenient clip-and-mail coupon to facilitate prospect response.

Envelope mailers, in their simplest form, consist of an outside envelope, letter and remittance envelope. The more elaborate ones include brochures or folders, and some of the gimmicky ones add such things as seed packets, unused stamps and miniature pencils.

Opinion varies on how best to handle each component in an envelope mailer, but the following guidelines have the most defenders.

Outside Envelope.   Use a #10 (4⅛" × 9½"), white, medium-stock quality, window, and print the regular name and address of your organization in the normal return-address position. Teaser copy (a statement on the front that makes a promise or otherwise piques interest) may or may not be a good idea. If you can come up with something exciting while avoiding overstatement, it should be helpful. Here's a simple teaser that worked well: "Inside . . . an important message for you from Billy Casper." Some authorities say you should not use a return address on the outside envelope. Their idea is to make the mailer look as much like a bill as possible, since almost everybody opens bills. There are two problems with this approach: (1) It violates at least the spirit of Better Business Bureau solicitation standards which rule out fund-raising literature made to look like bills. (2) The absence of a return address makes it impossible for the Postal Service to return incorrectly addressed letters to you. You can enlist the Postal Service in helping to update your address list by printing ADDRESS CORRECTION REQUESTED on the outside envelope just below the return address. If the address is incorrect, this notation—under rules in effect at this writing—tells the postman to do the following: (1) For letters under two ounces, write the correct address on the envelope and return it to you. If the correct address is not available, return the letter to you with a statement so signifying (MOVED-LEFT NO FORWARDING ADDRESS, etc.). (2) If the letter is over two ounces, return a form to you with the correct address or a statement declaring that the correct address is not available. This is a helpful service, but it has a price tag: you must pay for every envelope or form returned to you, even if no new address is available. The cost at this writing for each envelope or form is 25¢.

Letter. The lead is the most important part of a direct mail solicitation letter. If properly conceptualized and written, it will capture the reader's interest, make a promise of some kind and prepare him to receive your message and act on it. Here are 6 kinds of good leads for solicitation letters: *News:* Make an announcement of some kind ("Carterville's Boys' Club is building a new lodge, and you're invited to be part of it!"). *Narrative:* Plunge the prospect into a dramatic, interesting story ("On a chilly October evening in 1953, Virginia Stowe opened her front door and confronted a bedraggled, runaway boy who asked for a bowl of soup. He was the beginning of today's Stowe Homes for Boys"). *Question:* Involve and challenge the reader by asking a provocative question

("Do you know how many Freeburg girls won't be going to summer camp this year?"). *Itemization:* Use numbers to build credibility and get the prospect into your message ("Here are 12 practice-proved ways that Odyssey House helps kids with drug problems"). *Why/What/How:* Use a headline to answer questions your prospect could be expected to have about your organization ("How Wilson PTA Serves You and Your Child—And What to Expect in the Years Ahead"). *Startling Statement:* Grab the reader and almost force him to listen to what you have to say ("We're losing our minds!").

The body of the letter should build on the lead—amplify, prove, document, cite, enumerate. This is a good place to talk about *benefits* ("You'll have the satisfaction of knowing your gift is lifting young lives—today and in the years ahead"), and to marshal the support of outside spokesmen ("My seven years as Juvenile Court Judge have taught me that young people need a place to go where they feel comfortable . . . learn about themselves and others. That's why I enthusiastically support the club house campaign").

Use a general, "blanket" salutation ("Dear Friend," "Dear Little League Parent," etc.) if it seems right for your audience. If you're not comfortable with it (some fund-raisers feel that blanket salutations reek of insincerity), don't use a salutation—get right into the letter. The best approach, of course, is to use a personalized inside address and salutation ("Dear Mr. Johnson"), but this is time consuming and expensive if you are mailing to a hundred people or so and you do not have an automatic typewriter. We have all received letters in which the body has been printed and the inside address and salutation have been added by a typist in a matching face. Most people are "on" to this approach, and it's doubtful that the special effort involved is worth it.

The concluding paragraph of the letter should summarize your appeal, issue a clear call for action and convey a sense of urgency ("In short, Louis and his American Indian classmates need your help. And they need it *today*. Please take time *now*—while it's on your mind—to write out a check and return it in the envelope provided. Thanks!").

Some other guidelines for solicitation letters:

o Use short sentences, simple words and short paragraphs (six lines or less).
o Try for a conversational style that communicates warmth, openness, friendliness.
o Avoid superlatives and claims that challenge credibility.
o Leave no doubt about what you want.
o Remember that letters of almost any length—short, medium, long—are effective if they are well conceptualized and written.
o Arrange your thoughts so that they flow logically and easily from lead to conclusion.
o Always include a meaningful P.S.—these have high readership.

Solicitation letters for higher education, church, community service and health care are shown in Figures 4-16 through 4-21.

Brochures and Folders.

These are best used to *show* prospects—by means of illustrations, diagrams, photographs—why they should contribute to your cause. Too often brochures and folders are simply dressed-up extensions of letters—all blow (text) and no show (illustrations, etc.). A citizens' group seeking funds to cover two dangerous irrigation ditches had the right idea. They prepared a flyer to accompany their letter containing photographs of the exposed ditches and of two young children who had drowned in them. The flyer included a sketch detailing how the ditches would be covered.

A group seeking funds to build a college basketball arena also had the right idea. They prepared a folder giving the number and location of chair and bleacher seats. Each prospect was asked to pick out the chair seat he wanted, and to contribute $500 to reserve it for his lifetime.

If your project is one that doesn't require visual explanation (a college scholarship fund, for example), you can easily forgo a brochure or folder, and do your budget a big favor.

The guidelines for brochures, folders and special print media for in-person asking listed on pages 58 and 59 also apply to direct mail.

Remittance Envelope.

The remittance envelope is essential for two reasons: (1) It makes it convenient for the prospect to respond; (2) its backside carries the address label which shows through the outside envelope window. This label also serves to identify the donor when he mails the remittance envelope back to you with his contribution. (Not all donors write their return address on the remittance envelope. If they send cash rather than checks, the label is your only means of identifying them.)

If the remittance envelope is to be machine-stuffed into the outside envelope, make sure it's one inch shorter and at least one-quarter inch narrower than the outside envelope.

Some organizations print the equivalent of a contribution coupon on the inside flap of the remittance envelope. The donor is asked to supply the information requested, including current address, telephone number, employer (for matching gift purposes) and—if appropriate—how he wants his gift to be used. If you desire this information and you do not use the flap coupon, the best alternative is a separate coupon that the donor completes and slips into the remittance envelope with his contribution.

Most direct mail specialists feel that the remittance envelope should be postage prepaid (business reply), and extensive testing generally supports them. You pay, of course, only for those envelopes actually sent back to you. It might be well, however, for you to do some testing of your own: The difference in response with and without prepaid postage in your particular circumstance may not warrant the expense.

Always print your address on the remittance envelope in the normal address position. Also, use a colored stock—there is evidence suggesting that colored remittance envelopes have a higher return rate than white ones.

COMPUTER-ASSISTED TRANSLATION PROJECT	
PURPOSE:	DEVELOP A FAST, FAIRLY ECONOMICAL WAY TO TRANSLATE WRITTEN RUSSIAN, SPANISH, & FRENCH TO ENGLISH
ORGANIZATION:	TRANSLATION SCIENCE CENTER PERSONNEL
DIRECTOR:	J. DWIGHT JOHNSEN
LOCATION:	STATESBURG CAMPUS
SCHEDULE:	OCT 78 - COMPLETE LANGUAGE ANALYSIS
	JUL 80 - COMPLETE INITIAL PROGRAM
	JULY 81 - COMPLETE DETAILED PROGRAM
	DEC 82 - COMPLETE PRODUCTION MODEL
	JAN 84 - IMPLEMENT & REFINE
COST:	$2,450,000

Figure 4-1. Model Chart

RESULTS OF STUDY

This research is expected to supply the following information and data base specifications:

(a) A generalized specification for information flow and directory distribution in a distributed data base system.

(b) Generalized specifications for security techniques.

(c) Generalized specifications for query languages and techniques.

(d) A delineation of additional problems needing study and research in integrated distributed systems.

(e) A delineation of additional security problems needing further examination.

Figure 4-2.   Written Request Layout Sheet—Style A

o Another Castledale musical organization, Opera Workshop, recently presented Menotti's Amahl and the Night Visitors. Workshop students are now preparing another major production, Peter Pan, to be presented this spring.

o The College's traveling troupe of musicians and dancers--"Showcase Castledale"--involves 30 students from ten countries whose presentation is keyed to the theme, "Peace for All Nations through Stronger Families." Last year the troupe traveled 3,500 miles in giving 74 performances at schools, hospitals, and other institutions in the mountain states.

Unquestionably, Castledale has a rich, rewarding musical program. But the College, and the Music Department in particular, have pressing needs that cannot be met without the active, concerned involvement of alumni, corporations, foundations, and individuals.

Castledale College

Figure 4-3. Written Request Layout Sheet—Style B

REQUEST

Brigham Young University

Figure 4-4.   Solid-Front Cover for Written Request

VIDEODISC: CAUSING A COMMUNICATIONS
REVOLUTION IN EDUCATION

A REQUEST FOR FUNDING SUPPORT

The Development Office
Brigham Young University
Provo, Utah 84602

Figure 4-5.   Title Page for Written Request

SUMMARY

Castledale College and its Department of Continuing Education respectfully request your financial support in the amount of $4,600,000 to construct a self-contained continuing education complex that will handle present programs and future growth.

Full or partial funding is invited.

The Castledale continuing education program is now one of the largest in America, with registrations exceeding 225,000 annually. The program has quality as well as quantity, including pioneering programs in nutrition and nursing.

Unfortunately, the Department is caught in a critical space squeeze. Space for administrative functions is only about half of what it should be...regular College classroom space is not available at all during the regular school year... and the nearest hotel is miles away.

The complex, to be built on the south end of the campus, will consist of: Administrative Center ($1,400,000, 28,000 square feet), Conference Center ($2,600,000, 48,000 square feet), and Residence Center ($600,000, 17,000 square feet). Construction could begin as early as next spring if funding support were available.

The sections that follow present the need for the complex, plans to meet the need, budget, schedule, and other information to help you evaluate this request.

Figure 4-6.   Summary for Written Request

THE NEED

The lives of Americans are being increasingly
affected by scientific decisions. If we are to
have a proper measure of control over how we live,
and if we are to participate meaningfully in
public and private matters involving energy, resources, transportation, and health, we must
develop mature attitudes toward science.

General science courses at grade school through
university levels, developed many years ago to
meet the need for broadly based science education, have been helpful. But the crisis climate
of the Seventies, with its direct challenge to
scientific disciplines, has created an acute need
for greatly increased public awareness of science
in general and of sound in particular. Why
specifically sound? Because it is central to
so many other fields--language, music, speech,
psychology, biology, architecture, physics,
math--and thus provides a natural vehicle for
relevant science experiences.

The need for enhanced science education and the
reaction to it is everywhere evident--in the

Figure 4-7. Opening Paragraphs from Model—"The Need" Section

BUDGET

Expenses

Capital Expenses
Equipment . . . . $ 62,200
Farm House   35,000
Sheds   11,000
Land Clearing   20,000
Roads, Fences   29,000

Operating Expenses
Salaries (fulltime & students) . .   436,000
Utilities   35,000
Supplies (seeds, fuel, plants) . .   141,800
Hardware (lumber, wire, tools) . .   34,000
Depreciation   12,000

        Total Expenses . . . . $ 816,000

Revenue

Plot & Equipment Rentals . . . . . . $ 6,000
Crops
Beans   30,500
Peas   65,000
Lettuce   50,000

        Total Revenue . . . . $ 151,500

Balance to be Funded . . . . $ 664,500

Figure 4-8.   Budget for Written Request

PERSONNEL

J. Dwight Johnsen, associate professor of languages, is CSI project director. He is the author
of Computer-Aided Translation, the work upon which
the project is based. Dr. Johnsen received his
M.A. in German from Central College in 1961 and
his Ph.D. from the University of Illinois in 1970,
where he studied Slavic languages for three years
under a NDFL Fellowship. He joined the CC faculty
in 1967. Dr. Johnsen initiated computer-aided
translation research at CC in 1968. Since then he
has received three government contracts for research and development in language theory. He has
published over twenty articles in the professional
literature.

Thomas K. Steele, assistant to Dr. Johnsen, received his M.A. from Stanford University in
Chinese and his Ph.D. from Georgetown University
in Chinese and Linguistics. He lived for three
years in Taiwan and studied for two years in
Hong Kong under a NDFL Fellowship. Dr. Steele's
professional experience includes two years as head
of language instruction for the U. S. Defense Department and three years as a translator for
Internationale, Inc. He joined Central College in
1970. His publications include over a dozen
journal articles, papers at four symposiums, and
a book, New Insights Into Chinese Linguistic
Structure.

Figure 4-9. Model Personnel Resumes

WEBER STATE COLLEGE IN BRIEF

The College was founded at Ogden, Utah as Weber Stake Academy on January 7, 1889 by the Weber Stake Board of Education of The Church of Jesus Christ of Latter-day Saints. The 1933 Utah Legislature established Weber as a state junior college and placed it under control of the Utah State Board of Education.

In 1959 the Utah Legislature authorized upper division courses. Weber graduated its first senior class in 1963-64. The 1969 legislature created a Utah System of Higher Education and placed WSC under a State Board of Regents and an Institutional Council. WSC is the largest four-year baccalaureate degree-granting college in America.

President: Joseph L. Bishop, B.A., M.A., Brigham Young University, 1956, 1958; Ph.D., Claremont Graduate School and University Center, 1971.

Campus: 375 acres, 32 buildings, plant investment of more than $30 million. Over 88% of total building space has been built since 1960.

Faculty: 450 men and women representing a broad spectrum of local, state, national, and international backgrounds. About 200 hold doctoral degrees.

Students: Nearly 10,000 students representing 43 states and a dozen foreign countries.

Colleges: Baccalaureate degrees awarded in seven major schools with 32 departments and a Bachelor of General Studies. Associate degrees and one- and two-year curriculums offered in vocational and health fields. Quarter system: fall, winter, spring, and summer.

Figure 4-10.   Representative "In Brief" Listing

MEMBERSHIP APPLICATION

I want to promote athletics at Brigham Young University. Please enroll me as a member of the BYU Cougar Club.

Name _____   Address _____

City _____ State _____ Zip _____ Date _____

(Your Cougar Club contribution is a tax-exempt gift to the BYU Annual Alumni Fund and will be restricted to the Athletic Travel Fund for the purpose of recruiting athletes, according to NCAA and WAC regulations.)

Please accept my annual tax-deductible contribution of:

☐ $1,500 (Lifetime Member-
   ship; also payable @
   $500/year for three years)
☐ $500 (Golden Cougar)
☐ $100 (Regular Member)

☐ $25 (Associate Member,
   25 years of age and under)

☐ Check enclosed
☐ Bill me

Figure 4-11.   Coupon to Facilitate Prospect Response

⊙ PLEDGE CARD
THE DEVELOPMENT OFFICE

The Development Office
P.O. Box 7188 University Station
Provo, Utah 84602
(801) 374-1211, Ext. 2222

Gentlemen:

I hereby pledge to _____ the sum of $ _____ . I would like my contribution to

(check one) ☐ be used for general purposes   ☐ be restricted to _____ .

I have enclosed $ _____ , and I intend to pay any remaining balance as follows (check one):

☐ monthly   ☐ quarterly   ☐ semi-annually   ☐ annually

Name _____

Address _____

City _____ State _____ Zip _____

Signed _____ Date _____

Comments _____

_____

Figure 4-12.   Model Pledge Card

Castledale College
Wendover, Utah 84083

Thank you for your support of the annual fund in the amount of $_____.

Sincerely,_____
            Volunteer Worker

Amount enclosed $_____
(can be paid in installments)

Please make checks payable to Castledale College.

GIFT INSTRUCTIONS

☐ Use my gift where the need is greatest.
☐ Restrict my gift to_____.

Make all address corrections within the address box above.
Please return this completed slip with your contribution.

RECORD OF CALL

1. Total Amount Pledged: $_____
   (can be paid in installments)

   Gift Instructions:
   ☐ Use where need is greatest.
   ☐ Restrict gift to _____.

2. Call Back: ☐Line busy   ☐Not home

3. Unreachable: ☐Moved   ☐Wrong number
   ☐Deceased

4. Call Completed, Special Response:
   ☐Already gave
   ☐Does not wish to give this year

Figure 4-13.   Telefund Card

Charity is never lost: it may meet with
ingratitude, or be of no service to
those on whom it was bestowed, yet
it ever does a work of beauty and
grace upon the heart of the giver.

— Conyers Middleton, 1683–1750

THANKS

for the use of your phone and desk
last night.
I appreciated having a pleasant place
to work.

A volunteer worker for The Development Office, The Church of Jesus
Christ of Latter-day Saints

Figure 4-14.   "Thanks for Use of Your Desk" Table Tent

Castledale College
Wendover, Utah 84083

Frankly, we're worried.

If our records are correct, we have not yet received your
pledged contribution to Castledale College. And, unfortunately, time is running out. Our Silver Anniversary Fund
closes September 15th.

I hope you know that we do need your financial support, and
that your gift--large or small--is welcomed and needed. The
quality of Castledale's service in the years ahead will depend, in large measure, upon the support of those who
believe in us...people like you.

Please take time now--while you're thinking about it--to send
in your contribution.

All of us at CC appreciate your friendship and support.

Sincerely,

Brandon R. Ralphs

Brandon R. Ralphs, President

P.S. The premiere showing of CC's Silver Anniversary
motion picture, "From These Beginnings," will be held
August 21, 8 p.m., in Glendon Hall. Admission is free.
I hope you and your family will be able to attend.

Figure 4-15. Reminder Letter to Telefund Pledgees

OFFICE OF THE PRESIDENT

Someone once asked a successful fund-raiser if he ever flinched at asking for money. "I did once," he confessed, "when I wasn't personally convinced of the worth of the project for which I sought funds."

Fortunately, no one at Ricks College ever needs to flinch at asking for money for Ricks projects. <u>All</u> of them are worthwhile in the lives of young people.

Some projects, however, have a greater potential than others to reach people in a positive way beyond the campus and beyond the present generation. That's true of the College's campaign to raise $200,000 to buy a medium-sized pipe organ for the new fine arts building.

The students who become skilled organists as a result of being able to practice on this magnificent instrument will go forth throughout the world to touch the souls of men and women through music.

Please take a moment to read the accompanying folder--it gives complete details--and then use the enclosed reply card and envelope to make your contribution.

I know you'll feel good about it.

Sincerely,

Henry B. Eyring

Henry B. Eyring, President

P.S. Our Sixth Annual Piano Festival opens on April 9. You are cordially invited to attend.

Figure 4-16.   Solicitation Letter (Higher Education)

COMMUNITY CHRISTIAN CHURCH Harrisburg

Dear Brother & Sister Helms:

There are many ways to ask people for money. None of them,
though, is easy. But if your cause is just and you have a
special feeling for the people you ask--well, that can help
a lot.

As you probably heard in Sunday worship service earlier
this month, Community Christian Church needs your help if
it is to serve you better--more comfortably, more completely. Specifically, we would like to lay new carpet in
the chapel (you'll agree, we think, that it needs it)...
expand the scripture library (we're down to four Bibles!)
...and improve the sound system in the recreational hall
(and you thought it was your _ears_ all these years!).

Most of the members with whom we have spoken agree that
these improvements are important and worthwhile.

The total amount needed--based on the best estimates
available--is $5,700. That amount can quickly be raised
if you and every other member family will contribute $65.

Please accept this invitation to join with the other
member families in improving our worship facilities. You
can contribute in person at the Church or, if you prefer,
you can use the enclosed remittance envelope.

Thanks for all you do, in many different ways, to prosper
His work here in Harrisburg.

Sincerely,

Stanley C. Hawthorne

Stanley C. Hawthorne, Pastor

P. S. We hope that all contributions can be made within
sixty days so that the improvements will be complete in
time for our special Easter service.

Figure 4-17. Solicitation Letter (Church)

Dear Friend:

Today, right now, you can take a giant step for brotherhood.
Let me tell you about it.

In half-a-dozen programs on and off campus, BYU is waging
an exceptionally effective campaign to help the American
Indian...to give him hope and to break the ages-old pattern
of poverty, disease, and despair.

The techniques being used involve everything from educational
psychologists and soil scientists to one-ton tractors and
aerial maps.

On campus, the American Indian Education Department is giving
tailor-made assistance to 500 Indian students in three academic programs expressly designed for them. Off-campus, the
University's Institute of American Indian Services is helping
Indians in agriculture, tribal government, alcoholism education, small business development--and much more.

The spirit that characterizes all of these programs is an
abiding, consuming concern for the American Indians' spiritual
and temporal welfare.

The enclosed brochure tells the whole story. I hope you'll
read it thoughtfully. And, in a few days when a volunteer
worker calls and asks you for a pledge, I hope you'll take a
giant step for brotherhood by answering yes.

Thanks!

Donald T. Nelson
Director, The Development Office

P. S. In the event we're not able to reach you within the
next couple of weeks, we have enclosed a remittance envelope
for your convenience.

**Figure 4-18.   Solicitation Letter Used in Connection with a Telefund
Campaign (Higher Education)**

HANDICAPPED CHILDREN'S CENTER

It happens every year...

the people of Jacksonville respond generously to appeals for support from the Handicapped Children's Center.

Some give modest gifts, others large gifts. But most importantly, all seem to understand the Center's need for their help. Result: they do what they can.

My purpose in writing is to invite you to follow their example...to join with them in this vital, life-lifting work.

Your contribution will be gratefully received and acknowledged, and it will be used with maximum effectiveness to benefit the children involved.

Won't you take a moment now--this very day--to send in your contribution? A remittance envelope is enclosed for your convenience.

From all of us at the Center, and especially from the children, thanks!

Sincerely,

Harold Blakely

Harold "Ted" Blakely
Campaign Chairman

P. S. Our annual Open House will be held the week of July 11-15, from 10 to 3 each day. You and your family are cordially invited.

JACKSONVILLE

Figure 4-19. Solicitation Letter (Community Service)

RICKS
COLLEGE

Dear Ricks Alumnus:

If you have a moment, I'd like to talk to you about money.
About $3, specifically. $3 isn't very much. If you're like
me, you'll spend more than that within a day or two on an
innocent indulgence.

But if you and the 28,333 other Ricks College alumni contributed $3 to your alma mater, you could establish an $85,000
endowment for the David O. McKay Library.

It's a $3 investment that might be the best you'll ever
make because you'll become a "shareholder" in one of the
finest libraries to be found on any U. S. junior college
campus. Moreover, your $3 will make an enduring contri-
bution to the education of over 5,000 deserving young men
and women who are at Ricks today and who will be here tomorrow.

Then, too, your $3 gift will give you the special satisfac-
tion that comes with knowing you've given meaningful
assistance to a meaningful institution of higher learning--
a place and a people worthy of your support.

$3--won't you make it available now simply by writing out
your check and returning it in the enclosed envelope?

Please know that we're grateful for all you do--in many
ways--to further the programs of Ricks. If we haven't said
so lately, let us say so now: we appreciate you.

Sincerely,

Dewain Silvester

Dewain Silvester, President

P.S. If you can give more than $3, we can use it.

Figure 4-20.   Solicitation Letter (Higher Education)

UTAH VALLEY HOSPITAL
1034 North 500 West / Provo, Utah 84601

Hospitals are for helping.

You know that. But sometimes before hospitals can help, they
must be helped. That's the way it is right now for Utah
Valley Hospital. UVH is in the middle of a $19 million ex-
pansion program that will benefit you and those you love for
generations to come.

Specifically, the expansion will: * Increase floor space by
189,500 square feet. * Provide 203 new acute medical surgi-
cal patient beds, including a 24-bed intensive care unit.
* Provide an expanded emergency center and 18 outpatient
"holding beds." * Double the size of the radiology department and pharmacy. * Provide expanded parking.

The hospital's sponsor has arranged the bonding for most of
the funding. $4 million, however, must come from other
sources, including UVH employees and volunteers, medical
staff, businesses, and individual citizens--people like you.

Your contribution is essential if we are to raise the
$4 million.

How much should you give? That, of course, is your decision.
You know your individual circumstances best, but we respectfully suggest a minimum gift of $25.

I hope that you will help...that you will look upon this
appeal as an opportunity to invest in quality medical care
for yourself and for those you love.

Please send in your contribution soon.

Thanks!

Sincerely,

Mark J. Howard

Mark J. Howard
Executive Secretary, Fund-Raising Committee

P. S. A postage-paid, pre-addressed remittance envelope
is enclosed for your convenience.

Figure 4-21.   Solicitation Letter (Health Care)

Chapter Five

MODEL APPROACHES TO INDIVIDUALS, FOUNDATIONS AND CORPORATIONS

There are many different ways to approach the three fund-raising markets: individuals, foundations and corporations. Almost every fund-raiser has a favorite story about a far-out approach that worked (these have been known to evoke some belly-wrenching laughs at fund-raising conferences). The intent here, however, is to focus on those select, high-percentage-returns approaches that have the best chance of succeeding.

For the purposes of this chapter, let's assume that you are a successful, civic-minded citizen who has just accepted a request from the president of the Stevensville Boys' Club to raise $30,000 to add a gymnasium to the clubhouse.

You know that a broad-swath, mass appeal campaign is out. Such a campaign has already been conducted in Stevensville. It involved a telefund, fund-raising projects by the boys (car washing, grass cutting), and a door-to- door campaign by club leaders and volunteers. Total yield: $12,700. The $30,000 you must raise is needed in *addition* to the $12,700.

The paragraphs that follow describe how you might best approach individuals, foundations and corporations on behalf of the Stevensville Boys' Club—or any similar organization. In each instance it is assumed that you have completed the appropriate preliminary steps described in Chapter 3.

INDIVIDUALS

From your prospect file you should select six or seven individuals who seem promising, because of (1) wealth, (2) interest in youth (sports, outdoor recreation, scouting, etc.), (3) past giving patterns, (4) tax situation, and (5) strong community ties.

Your first step is to talk with people who can give you current, reliable information about the prospects. When you approach them, be aboveboard about your intent: "Dr. Green, I'm considering asking Mr. Baird to make a large contribution to the Boys' Club. I need your help, though, in getting some information about him. Would you mind answering a few questions for me?" If Dr. Green declines, others will not, and eventually you'll be able to ask questions like these:

○ Is Mr. Baird's financial condition still sound?
○ I know he has some stock plus land on the beach, but are you aware of any other assets?
○ He has supported the Boys' Club for several years with small gifts. Do you know if he has any other charitable interests?
○ Has he ever said anything to you about how he intends to use his wealth?
○ Can you give me the names of some of his other friends?
○ Would you say that Mr. Baird has an average or above average need for social recognition?

After you have investigated the other prospects, let's say that Mr. Baird turns out to be the most promising. From Dr. Green and others you learn that Mrs. Baird is deceased, and that the couple's two children are both financially successful in their own right.

You also learn that Mr. Baird has spoken favorably about community programs to help the disadvantaged, especially young people. You make two important discoveries about his financial situation: (1) He recently sold some of his land and faces a stiff capital gains tax, and (2) he holds several hundred shares of stock purchased several years ago through an employee stock plan. You learn that Mr. Baird is about average in his need for social recognition, and you are told his best friend is Fred Driggs.

Visit with Fred Driggs for additional insights. Be careful to avoid any suggestion that you are inviting him to join with you in a "plot" involving his best friend. Mr. Driggs may be reserved in his responses, but he will likely verify the accuracy of your information—and add a fact or two. Do *not* ask him to keep your meeting confidential. It may be to your advantage to have him alert Mr. Baird to your intentions. (Actually, as discussed in Chapter 3, carefully letting the prospect know that you intend to ask for a gift is a necessary part of the cultivation process. If the prospect is totally surprised when you ask, your cultivation effort has fallen short.)

By now you have cleared all of the necessary hurdles, and the race begins in earnest. Call Mr. Baird and arrange an appointment with him. Lunch at his favorite restaurant (which Fred Driggs identified for you) is a good format. Your telephone conversation might go something like this:

> "Mr. Baird? My name is _____ . . . I don't believe you know me. I'm working with the Stevensville Boys' Club on a fund-raising project. I know of your interest in young people and their problems, and I want very much to meet with you and discuss the Boys' Club building program. I think you'll find it interesting and worthwhile. Could we get together sometime soon at Bratton's—my schedule is open . . . what would work best for you?"

Give careful thought to whether or not someone besides you and Mr. Baird should attend the luncheon meeting. For example, if Mr. Baird is likely to make the gift in deferred form, such as a charitable remainder trust, you should seriously consider having an attorney attend. Realize, though, that involving an attorney might be perceived as presumptuous by Mr. Baird. Consequently, carefully weigh all the factors involved. Also consider the possibility of having someone else—an individual held in high esteem by Mr. Baird—present your case. Again, weigh the factors, then act. Whatever you decide, *spring no surprises on Mr. Baird.*

If you plan to go to the meeting without an attorney, consult with one to determine how Mr. Baird can best make the gift from a tax standpoint. (The attorney may well advise Mr. Baird to give the Boys' Club $30,000 worth of his stock. This approach will enable him to avoid paying capital gains tax for which he would be liable if he sold the stock—the situation he faces with the land sale. In addition, Mr. Baird will be able to claim a charitable tax deduction on his tax return, and reduce the amount of federal estate tax that will eventually come due on his property.)*

From discussions with the Boys' Club president and governing board, determine in advance of the luncheon whether or not they are prepared to name the gymnasium after Mr. Baird. This question inevitably comes up, so be prepared for it.

At the meeting, use the in-person asking technique and tools described in Chapter 4.

Mr. Baird will probably tell you one of three things: (1) "Yes, I will give the Stevensville Boys' Club $30,000"; (2) "I want to help the Boys' Club, but $30,000 is more than I want to give. I'll give you $____"; (3) "No, I'm sorry, I am not in a position to help." If Mr. Baird responds with (1) or (2), implement the steps described in Chapter 6. If he responds with (2) or (3), do not move to the next market (foundations); rather, move to the next best individual prospect on your original list. Why? *Individuals* with strong local ties are the best of all possible prospects.

FOUNDATIONS

Foundations as a whole are something of an American mystery, so, first, some background. There are about 26,000 grant-making foundations in the U.S., and they are believed to control $26 billions. No one knows their exact wealth at any given moment, because their portfolios fatten and flatten with the vagaries of the economy.

---

* Tax-planned giving is complex, so rely on legal counsel. Publications to help acquaint you with the subject are available from several firms. Refer to Chapter 11.

Dwight McDonald's definition of one particular foundation (Ford) is memorable: ". . . a large body of money completely surrounded by people who want some."[1]

But F. Emerson Andrews' definition is the most meaningful: ". . . nongovernmental, nonprofit, has a principal fund of its own, is managed by its own trustees and directors, is established to maintain or aid social, educational, charitable, religious or other activities serving the common welfare."[2]

Foundations are predominantly an American phenomenon. Of those among the world's 25 richest, only five are non-United States, and of the 315 with assets above $10 million, 95 percent are American.[3]

Basically, there are five kinds of foundations:

○ *General Purpose.*   These are among the biggest, best known, and most prestigious. They support a wide range of projects and have comparatively few grant-making restrictions. Typically, they tackle the toughest problems of the age.

○ *Special Purpose.*   They make grants only to (1) a specific field, (2) a well-delineated activity, or (3) a certain geographical area. Their names often indicate their field of interest: Foundation for Child Development, Police Foundation, etc.

○ *Corporate/Company Foundations.*   These act as philanthropic "agents" for business organizations. Legally, they are independent entities expressly created for giving. Company officers ordinarily serve as trustees. Usually, they give in communities in which their founding firms have plants.

○ *Family Foundations.*   They are large in number but—with some notable exceptions—small in assets. Although they are under the control of families that establish them, they give to a wide range of causes. *Don't sell them short*, especially if they are located in your own community.

○ *Community Foundations.*   These are made up of many small funds under centralized, community management, and are funded by living donors, endowments, bequests, family foundations and open-end trusts. They usually restrict their grants by geographical area and donor interest. An excellent—and growing —source of support for certain projects.

For you as a fund-raiser, though, what matters most is that the Foundation Center (888 Seventh Avenue, New York, N.Y. 10019) publishes an authoritative tome known as *The*

Foundation Directory. The fifth edition (1975) lists 2,533 foundations. These are the ones that merit your attention: They account for 90 percent of the assets of United States foundations and for 80 percent of all United States foundation giving.*

The Foundation Directory may not be the best guide to the foundation market (at least one commercially available publication is kept more up to date), but it's probably the least expensive. In any event, without the Directory or its commercial equivalent, you have little chance of successfully raising foundation funds on behalf of the Stevensville Boys' Club— or any other organization. The Directory is available in many public libraries, and contains the following foundation data:

○ Names and addresses in alphabetical order by state.
○ Purpose and activities.
○ Financial data, including assets, expenditures, number of grants made and dollar value of highest and lowest grants.
○ Name of the donor, trustees, officers and person with whom you should correspond (sometimes this information is incomplete).

Other valuable resources for approaching foundations:

○ The Foundation Center (at address previously listed). A complete, comprehensive source of foundation information. The Center, a nonprofit educational organization, maintains libraries in New York, Washington, D.C. and Chicago, as well as regional collections in nearly 40 states. Materials available include an exhaustive collection of foundation-oriented books, documents, microfiche and reports. Files are maintained on over 26,000 foundations.
○ *Foundation News.* It appears every other month as a kind of foundations house organ. The *News* will apprise you of current foundation concerns (editorials and articles such as "Liberating the Handicapped" are regular features), personnel changes, and new publications. A special feature is the Foundation Grants Index, "a record of currently reported foundation grants of $5,000 and more." The index lists grants made and amount, by foundation and recipients. It is available in many libraries, or you can

---

* The sixth edition, published in the fall of 1977, lists 2,818 foundations. The percentages describing their assets and grant-making are unchanged.

subscribe by writing Box 783, Old Chelsea Station, New York, N.Y. 10011.

○ *Annual Reports.*   These are indispensable if you want an in-depth understanding of a particular foundation—what it is doing, thinking, planning. The reports are sometimes available by writing the foundation involved. If that fails, try the extensive annual report file of the Foundation Center.

○ *Computer Searches.*   These are commercially available and, beyond question, extremely helpful in certain circumstances.

Now, back to the Stevensville Boys' Club. When you get your hands on *The Foundation Directory,* turn to the "Index of Fields of Interest" at the back. The special interests of over 800 of the foundations listed in the Directory proper appear here. At least six headings should draw your interest: Child Development, Child Welfare, Children, Community Funds, Youth and Youth Agencies. You will find references to over 280 foundations under these six headings—and you still need to check the interests of foundations not listed in this index who give exclusively in your state.*

Give special attention to the "Community Funds" heading. Invariably, foundations with an interest in community funds are *corporate foundations.* Because Stevensville is located near a company with a corporate foundation, you are in an enviable position to approach that foundation. This is true for at least two reasons: (1) Corporate foundations are unabashedly interested in building community goodwill for their founding firms, and (2) frequently, the firm's employees will directly benefit from the proposed project. Case in point: A hospital in a Utah community was seeking funds for a multimillion dollar expansion program. The management of a large corporation located nearby was interested in the hospital expansion, because it was seen as vital to adequate health care for their employees—and for a planned expansion of its own. Management also wanted to be a "good neighbor" in

---

* Foundations that limit their grant-making to the city or state in which they are located are not referenced in the "Index of Fields of Interest." Their interests are listed only in the body of the Directory, along with the other information about them. You can quickly identify these foundations, however, by means of the "Index of Foundations by State and City," also in the back of the Directory.

the community, and suggested that the hospital's fund-raising director approach the corporate foundation and ask for $1 million. He did, and he got it!

Let's assume now that you have identified, researched and settled on at least one promising foundation prospect. In the process you have assured yourself of the following:

○ Stevensville Boys' Club is within the foundation's area of interest.
○ The foundation does support brick-and-mortar type projects. (Most foundations do not—they give only for research or programs.)
○ The foundation is not prohibited by its charter from giving in your state or city.
○ The amount of money you seek is within the foundation's customary giving range.

What next? Ideally, arrange an interview with an officer of the foundation. An interview is especially helpful if you do not know the foundation well. Make the attempt by phone or letter. The former is best, but sometimes difficult. Persistence is the key. In seeking an interview appointment, couch your project in terms of the *foundation's* interests ("This project, Mr. ____, is consistent with your foundation's interests, concerns and past patterns of philanthropic support"). Avoid too many specifics, anything controversial and hard sell. Drop names if you can do so legitimately. Better still, have someone who is well known to the foundation ask for the appointment. A word of caution here, though: *Never* go over a foundation officer's head. To do so is a direct affront to his authority and position, and he won't forget it.

If you are *not* granted an interview, you should still end up ahead—with valuable additional insights into your foundation prospect. Refusals are almost always delivered with some helpful words of illuminating explanation.

If you *are* granted an interview, go to it well prepared. If you are not thoroughly knowledgeable about project details, take along someone who is. Almost without exception, those closest to a project speak the most compellingly and convincingly for it (even if they seem to be nearly incoherent on other subjects!).

The purpose of the interview is about the same as the purpose of the opening round of a boxing match: to introduce the combatants and prepare them for the give and take that follows. For this reason, you usually don't ask for the grant in the interview, and you don't leave the written request. Instead, you listen, learn, "fish" and incorporate your new knowledge into the presentation to be made later.

After the interview, it is unlikely that you will be invited back to make the presentation in person (the foundation officer's time is the problem). But if you are, keep it short, straightforward and allow ample time for questions. Use simple, highly functional communication tools, such as the charts described in Chapter 4. Leave the written request, prepared in accordance with the outline given in Chapter 4 and tailored to reflect what you learned in the interview. Again, involve in the meeting those most knowledgeable about your project.

If you are not invited to make the presentation in person, submit your written request by mail with a cover letter. Make the letter warm but businesslike. Express appreciation for the interview, and address the letter to the person who interviewed you. Include a copy of your annual report if one is available.

A model cover letter is shown in Figure 5-1.

Many foundations suggest that your first contact with them should be in the form of a one- or two-page "letter of inquiry." This advice is typically worded as follows: "Applicants are asked to send a letter to the foundation which includes a brief description of the project, what it is designed to do and any other relevant background information. If the foundation is interested in receiving a full proposal, it will so advise the applicant." Presumably, an interview appointment and a chance to present your proposal would then follow.

You may, indeed, want to take this advice. On the other hand, if you use the request format described in Chapter 4, you have, in effect, the same thing as a "letter of inquiry" (the summary) plus some helpful backup information that may well have more persuasive power and impact than a letter alone could ever have. Part of the secret is to stand out from the crowd, and let's face it—it's tough to do that if you're held to a two-page letter!

In case you're wondering if some foundations provide application forms that you merely fill in and submit—much like applying for a government grant—the answer is, with very few exceptions, no.

If you're applying to a large foundation, one of its officers will probably acknowledge receipt of your request within two weeks or so. If you are applying to a small to medium-sized foundation, especially if it does not have a full-time staff, you may never hear anything (really!). If more than a month goes by without any word, query the foundation by letter or phone.

Even if it looks like the Stevensville Boys' Club is going to receive a foundation grant, don't schedule any basketball games right away. Some foundations meet as infrequently as once a year to act on requests! Remember, too, that if you do receive a grant, it may not be for the full $30,000. Consequently, keep your options open.

Finally, a few words about foundations and direct mail. Let's assume that in your research you uncovered 30 or 40 foundations that seemed to be fairly good prospects—not outstanding, but worth a modest try. You can't afford to visit them in person, and you don't feel they merit a full-blown written request. The answer? Direct mail. Send them a simple folder or brochure and a cover letter. Some foundations will not respond to direct mail appeals, and they say so in the *Foundation Directory*. But others will, and they are worth a try. One university sent out a mail appeal to nearly 200 foundations. Only one responded—with a $50,000 grant.

CORPORATIONS

Unlike foundations, corporations are not in business to give their money away. In fact, corporations are not at all charitable in the classical sense of the word. Charity requires that one gives his *own* money away. When corporations give to charity, however, they are giving their *shareholders'* money away. Irving Kristol, who writes for the *Wall Street Journal*, explains the special responsibility this entails: "When you give away your own money, you can be as foolish, as arbitrary, as whimsical as you like. But when you give away your stockholders' money, your philanthropy must serve the longer-term interests of the corporation. Corporate philanthropy should not be, cannot be disinterested."[4]

Little wonder then that corporate giving is heavily involved in "enlightened self-interest." And even so, the scope of such giving is only a fraction of what it might be. Most companies give little or nothing. Of 1.7 million corporations filing tax returns in 1970, only 20 percent reported charitable gifts, and only six percent gave over $500. A handful of big corporations do most of the giving.[5]

What does all this mean for you and the Stevensville Boys' Club (or a college, hospital or similar organization)? Simply this: Corporations are the *least* promising of your prospects. Approach them last, and concentrate on those that stand to gain by giving to you. That gain may involve public relations, community goodwill, helpful sales contacts—any number of solid, good-for-business factors.

Look around Stevensville. Pick out the six or seven biggest, most prosperous businesses. Read their annual reports. Study their organization charts. Learn the names and backgrounds of their top executives. Find out who handles their charitable requests. The president? Vice-president? Committee? Corporate giving officer? Public relations director? (Big companies have special departments for this purpose. One oil company, for example, has a "manager of community development"; another, a "corporate contributions counselor.")

Review the companies' past giving patterns. You will find that some give only to higher education—on the theory that they are obligated to support the institutions that educate their work force. This support takes many forms, including research grants, scholarships and fellowships, endowment grants and work-study programs. You will find that others make cash grants to worthy community projects, and that still others give equipment and material assistance to a variety of institutions.

Zero in on two or three prime prospects by asking yourself the following questions:

○ Will this company be able to consider its contribution as an investment that will return tangible dividends—community goodwill, improved employee morale, "good neighbor" image, positive publicity, etc.?

○ Is the company at this moment in special need of a public relations "coup" because of labor unrest, a disquieting disclosure, environmental incident, recent reduction in force, etc.?

○ Does my project align philosophically or materially with the products or services of this company? (If so, you should strongly consider approaching the company for a contribution of those services or products. For example, you might ask the Stevensville Brick Foundry to contribute bricks; Stevensville Plumbing, to contribute the plumbing work; Stevensville Roofing, the roof; etc.).

○ Do this company's employees stand to benefit directly from the gymnasium? For example, will children of the workers be using the gym?

After you have identified your best corporate prospects, face up to this fact: It's highly unlikely that any one of them is going to give you $30,000. Few companies want to set that kind of precedent, because it would open them up to other organizations' requests that they could not honor. (In the case of a public company, there's also the matter of stockholder relations.) For these reasons, you must assign a *realistic* quota to each company. Firm quota guidelines are not likely to be reliable, so you must consider the individual circumstances of each company. Is it sound? Are its prospects bright? Does it have strong local ties? Has it demonstrated a sense of "corporate citizenship" in the past? If it has given to community projects, how much did it give? Is its top management friendly to the Boys' Club? Whatever figure you arrive at, it probably shouldn't be more than $10,000. Again, though, individual circumstances must dictate.

Use the in-person asking technique and tools. As in the case of foundations, take along those who can best speak for your cause. Also, try to involve at least one influential member of the community in your presentation. Don't be bashful about revealing what other companies in the community are doing, especially if they are competitors and their gifts are good ones. Quite often, for example, a bank giving officer will not commit to a specific amount until he knows what other banks are giving. For this reason, go first to your very best prospect within a given business field and try to get him to give a precedent-setting gift.

The post-asking suggestions in Chapter 6 relate primarily to individuals. Some, however, are adaptable to corporations. Apply them as appropriate.

For relatively small companies and those that are not prime prospects, here are two other possibilities: (1) A door-to-door campaign involving an adult volunteer and one of the boys, and (2) direct mail. If you use the latter, make your appeal as personal as possible. Since you will not be mailing to a large number of companies, individually type and personalize each letter. Keep the mailer simple so that you can hold down production costs (otherwise, you run the risk of not recovering your investment, to say nothing of failing to make a "profit").

NOTES

1. Merrimon Cuninggim, *Private Money and Public Service* (New York: McGraw-Hill Book Company, 1972), p. 137.
2. Warren Weaver, *U.S. Philanthropic Foundations* (New York: Harper and Row, 1967), p. 39.
3. Joseph Dermer, *How to Raise Funds from Foundations* (Public Service Materials Center, 1975), p. 13.
4. *Wall Street Journal*, March 21, 1977.
5. *Giving in America*, Report of the Commission on Private Philanthropy and Public Needs, 1975, p. 154.

BOYS'CLUB OF UTAH COUNTY

Mr. Julius Bergen
Chairman of the Board
Max C. Fleischmann Foundation
P. O. Box 1871
Reno, Nevada 89505

Dear Mr. Bergen:

President Crandall and I enjoyed the opportunity to meet with you last week to discuss plans for our new club house. It was kind of you to take the time to see us.

I am pleased to enclose our proposal to the Fleischmann Foundation for a $50,000 grant to the Utah County Boys' Club to assist with construction of the club house.

My associates and I sincerely believe that such a grant would be a sound investment in our community, benefiting hundreds of young men for generations to come.

We hope that you will give our proposal careful, thoughtful consideration.

If I can help by answering questions you may have, making arrangements for you to visit the construction site, or in some other way, please call on me.

Thank you again for your interest and concern.

Very truly yours,

Alan R. Robinson
Executive Director

Figure 5-1. Cover Letter for Request to Foundation

Chapter Six

AFTER YOU ASK

W hether your prospect's answer is "yes" or "no," your job isn't over once you've asked. In fact, it's just begun! This chapter describes the important steps you should take after you get your answer.

IF THE ANSWER IS "YES"

Obviously, the first thing you should do is to express your appreciation to the donor. But how is that best done? A telephone call? Letter? Personal visit?

The answer depends on the amount of money the donor has contributed. Although a small thank-you can be every bit as sincere and meaningful as a large thank-you, it ultimately comes down to what is appropriate. Large gifts require more than simple expressions of appreciation—both recipient and donor usually recognize this fact.

The paragraphs that follow present thank-you guidelines for four levels of giving: $100,000 and up, $25,000 to $100,000, $10,000 to $25,000 (defined herein as the "upper levels" of giving) and $1 to $10,000 (defined herein as the "lower level" of giving). These guidelines not only give you a blueprint for appropriate action, they also help to ensure that Donor Y who gives you $15,000 receives about the same treatment as Donor Z who gives you $15,000. Remember that they are only guidelines, and that you should adapt them as individual circumstances dictate.

Remember, too, that you should record, receipt and acknowledge *every* gift, regardless of its size. You should do so to promote sound fund-raising management, accurate reporting (for internal and governmental purposes) and authentic tax documentation for your donors. The combined Thank You/This Is Your Receipt form (Figure 6-1) is an efficient, economical way to accomplish all three functions. Prepare the form in duplicate so that you will have a copy for your files. Note that the form shown in Figure 6-1 makes a point of the fact that individual acknowledgment of every gift is prohibitively expensive, so "we hope you will accept this communication as a simple but sincere expression of our gratitude." This statement is aimed, of course, at those donors whose gifts are modest and who will not receive a personalized acknowledgement.

Fund-raisers sometimes puzzle over how much to spend on thank-you activities. National practice suggests 1½ percent to 3 percent of the contribution. For example, a $10,000 gift would suggest a $150 to $300 expenditure.

$100,000 and Up

Assume that Mr. L. W. Bird has given your institution $200,000 to establish a scholarship fund. Clearly, a letter or telephone call is an inappropriate way to say thanks. Mr. Bird should receive a visit—by appointment—from the president, director or chief executive of your institution (hereafter "president") and key officers. They should take that opportunity to thank Mr. Bird in a warm, sincere, enthusiastic way. They should look him in the eye, shake his hand and make no bones about how pleased they are. (If Mr. Bird lives several hundred miles away, then a visit by a representative of your institution would be appropriate. He should personally present a letter from your president to Mr. Bird. If Mr. Bird is not available for a personal visit within a month after the gift is received, then a letter from the president should be sent. It should, however, be followed by a personal visit as soon as circumstances permit.)

Mr. Bird should be told that your institution wants to honor him at a luncheon, dinner, faculty meeting or in some other appropriate fashion. Ideas should be presented to Mr. Bird for his consideration, then adapted to conform with his wishes. Some donors are uncomfortable in the limelight. Consequently, you should be prepared to opt for a small, quiet get-together for lunch or dinner. Others will feel differently, and will forthrightly tell you so. Some will present you with a 500-name guest list for an announcement and appreciation banquet at the Hotel Ritz ballroom to be attended by your state's entire congressional delegation! If you're smart, you'll smile and tell them you think that's a marvelous idea. Then you'll set to work to make it a truly memorable event.

If the donor does decide on some kind of public event, you must work closely with him or his representative to see that his wishes are met. Questions to be resolved include the following: Who is to be invited? Who is to speak? Where is the event to be held? Is the gift to be announced at the event or before the event? (If the former approach is taken, are news media representatives to be invited?)

The event should include distribution of a booklet commemorating the donor's gift. The booklet should include a brief biography and photographs of the donor (family album photos showing the donor and his family through the years are excellent), and an explanation of how the gift will benefit those served by your institution. Such booklets are not only effective in paying tribute to the donor, they are also effective as cultivational literature to encourage other prospects to make similar gifts. Representative cover, page layout, and paragraphs from such booklets that have been nationally recognized for excellence are presented in Figures 6-2, 6-3, and 6-4.

Within a week after the event has been held, the president should send Mr. Bird a letter that again thanks him for his gift, refers to favorable comments that have been received and sets the tone for a mutually rewarding future relationship. A suggested letter is shown in Figure 6-5. Ideally, the form in Figure 6-1 should not be sent to donors at the upper giving levels until this letter and the other personalized thank-you procedures have been completed.

If all of this seems like a lot of trouble, ask yourself how long it would take you and your staff to earn the $200,000 that Mr. Bird contributed to your institution, the thousands of additional dollars that he may contribute in the future and the thousands of other dollars that may be contributed by others stimulated by Mr. Bird's example.

Avoid the time-worn practice of awarding plaques, desk sets, paperweights and similar off-the-shelf items to donors at the upper giving levels. These are not likely to make a good impression. Try, instead, to select unique gifts tailored to each donor's background and interests. One university, for example, gave a Navajo-made quartz chess set to a donor who had established a scholarship fund for American Indian students. And a hospital administrator whose institution had received a large cash donation from a broadcasting executive gave the donor an antique radio. A brass plate affixed to it carried an appropriate inscription.

$25,000 to $100,000

At this level, too, a personal visit is entirely appropriate, although a presidential letter will probably suffice. You should remember, however, that some donors will contribute relatively modest amounts initially to an institution to see how well they are received. If the reaction is a positive and appreciative one, they give additional gifts in larger amounts. Frankly, under such circumstances, a personal visit, in addition to being a thoughtful gesture, may well be an excellent investment.

Luncheons, dinners or other special events honoring donors at this level are proper; however, they should not be large affairs. The rule here is quality on a small scale. A dinner at a fine restaurant involving the president, one or two other executives, and the donor and his family would be entirely in order. Many donors are justifiably put off when institutions spend lavishly on frills. Institutions who do so may unwittingly demonstrate that they are financially irresponsible. That, of course, is the one message you don't want your donors to get.

Here, too, a warm letter that sets the tone for a good future relationship is appropriate about a week or so after the thank-you event is held (Figure 6-5).

Some donors who give at this level—and, indeed, at other levels as well—will tend to feel they "own" your institution. A small minority will attempt to capitalize on your sense of obligation to them by demanding certain privileges, special treatment and other trappings of power and influence. If you are too eager in responding to these demands, you may be inviting still other demands. Consequently, it is important to establish a written policy stating what you are and are not willing to do to accommodate donors beyond the initial thank-you event. The development offices of some colleges and universities, for example, routinely purchase block seating at football and basketball games for donors and prospective donors. This is a reasonable service that most institutions can comfortably provide. To attempt to provide certain other kinds of services, however, might clearly be inappropriate. Case in point: One donor asked to have use of a university's ballroom one night a month throughout the school year. Quite properly, his request was denied.

$10,000 to $25,000

For moderate to large fund-raising organizations (those raising $1 million or more annually), this is probably the lowest giving level that merits special treatment. The donor should receive a letter of thanks from the president and an invitation to lunch or some other low-key get-together.

Don't overlook on-site opportunities to inform donors better about your work and to entertain and involve them. A doctor at one hospital, for example, demonstrated an exciting new diagnostic tool to a donor—a brain-scanning machine. The donor was so impressed that he gave a follow-up gift of several thousand dollars to purchase needed accessories for the scanner.

You can involve donors at the upper giving levels in many

mutually rewarding ways. Almost without exception, donors who can afford to give at these levels have something worthwhile to say—about their business, about the economy, about values, about lessons they have learned. Many institutions—especially those in higher education—wisely involve these people in guest lectureships, panel discussions, demonstrations, committee assignments (including chairmanships) and in other service-oriented capacities. Be careful, of course, about asking donors to serve in ways that would give them unwarranted control over their own financial contributions.

$1 to $10,000

How you thank donors at this level depends on the size of your organization and its relationship with them. Many large fund-raising organizations do not give special acknowledgement (such as a presidential letter) for gifts of under $10,000. However, for some organizations, a gift of $5,000 or even $2,000 is a major windfall—perhaps the biggest they will ever receive. Consequently, if the gift is a big one for *your* organization, thank the donor in the way that seems most appropriate. That may mean a personal visit, it may mean lunch or dinner, it may mean a presidential letter and it may mean all three.

Donors at this level who give to moderate to large fund-raising organizations should, in most cases, not receive more than the Thank You/This Is Your Receipt form (Figure 6-1). There are two exceptions, however.

The first exception involves gifts, donors or causes that are unique and worthy of special recognition. For example, the president of a college in a small town was greeted one afternoon by 20 high school students who gave him a bank bag containing $627 in cash. The students explained that the money was for the library addition the college was struggling to build. Since they planned to enroll soon at the college and use the library, the students wanted to do their part. Clearly, such a gift merits special recognition—perhaps a news story in the local paper plus lunch with the president and library director.

The second exception involves gift clubs. Membership in such clubs is awarded to donors who give at certain established levels, usually on an annual basis. For example, at a typical college a donor becomes a member of the Old Main Society with an annual contribution of $200; a member of the President's Club for an annual contribution of $500; and a lifetime member of the President's Club for a one-time contribution of $8,000. Membership is usually awarded automatically—not as a result of a specific request by the donor. Benefits of club membership typically include an annual banquet, quarterly newsletter and plaque or certificate. One of the most important benefits, however, is the satisfaction donors derive from associating with a recognized, respected group. The "benefits" offered by gift clubs are, in reality, thank-you events. Make certain that you follow through with them, so that your donors receive what you promised in your initial membership announcement.

Some fund-raisers justify a relatively high thank-you expenditure for gift clubs—say 5 percent or 10 percent above regular fund-raising overhead—on the ground that special expressions of appreciation will bear fruit later in the form of larger contributions and, eventually, bequests. You may also be inclined to use this rationale. Remember, however, that the credibility of your entire program can be negatively affected by overspending on thank-you events that are, after all, highly visible and therefore especially susceptible to public disenchantment.

Other Post-Gift Guidelines

Because past donors are your best prospects for future gifts, you should do more than thank them. You should initiate and maintain an ongoing cultivation program for them.

Donors at the higher giving levels should receive invitations to events in their areas of interest. At the beginning of each school year, for example, one large university sends donors interested in drama an announcement of plays scheduled for that year. The donors are asked to check the plays they would like to attend, and tickets are sent to them at the appropriate time. Another university keeps a file on donors with engineering backgrounds and involves them extensively in activities held during its annual engineering week.

It's also a good idea to put upper-level donors on distribution lists for publications and other materials in which they could be expected to have an interest. In fact, some institutions produce newsletters, magazines and special reports expressly for donor cultivation. Typically, these publications report projects in progress, successes to date and what could be accomplished if additional funding were available.

Large file cards containing data that will facilitate the cultivation of past donors are extremely helpful. Such cards should be prepared and maintained for all donors at the upper three giving levels. A suggested format is shown in Figure 6-6.

The names of donors at the lower giving level who consistently say "yes" to direct mail or other mass appeals should be placed in a "preferred donor" file and solicited differently than the others. This is important for two reasons.

First, because they are loyal givers, there is no reason for you to spend time and money on multiple contacts. One contact a year—a reminder—is usually all they need. You should, however, inform them of this fact: tell them that because they have established themselves as loyal supporters, you will contact them only once a year (or at least less than you have been doing). Most will appreciate the fact that this approach reduces your overhead and increases the effectiveness of their contribution. A letter to announce and explain this approach is shown in Figure 6-7.

Second, such a file will enable you readily to identify donors who are good prospects for larger gifts, including membership in gift clubs such as a president's or director's club. Fund-raisers at a large Midwestern university noticed, for example, in reviewing their "preferred donor" file, that one alumna had been contributing consistently for many years, and that her contributions were large. They researched the woman's background and not only discovered that she had substantial wealth, but also that she had a retarded child. They arranged to meet with her, and the eventual result was a $300,000 contribution to the university's center for learning-disabled children.

IF THE ANSWER IS "NO"

If your prospect says "no," the worst thing you can do is to give up. By all means, try again—preferably within six months. Timing is critical to the success of charitable requests, especially those at the upper giving levels. Just because a prospect turns you down today doesn't mean that he will turn you down six months from now. His stock may be down. He may have just made a gift to another charitable institution. His liquid assets may be at a premium at the moment. He may wish to check you out before he makes any kind of commitment. There are many reasons why prospects say no, and very few of them are not susceptible to change.

The more you ask a given prospect, the better your chances of success. Most prospects find it difficult, even embarrassing, to say no more than three or four times, especially if the same person does the asking each time.

You should maintain a file card on all upper-level individuals you ask, whether you are asking them as individuals or representatives of a company or foundation. The card should list the date they were asked, amount requested, who did the asking and the prospect's response. Without such a card, you have no sure guide for follow-up action.

Is there ever a time when you should give up on a prospect? Yes—when he tells you firmly that he isn't interested or requests that you not contact him further.

Two years or more of "no" responses from individuals at the lower giving levels solicited by direct mail, in telefunds or in other mass appeals suggests that you should give them a low solicitation priority. Specifically, you should contact them less often and devote less time and money to them. For example, if you are soliciting individuals at the lower giving levels three times a year by direct mail, you should consider contacting your "no" people only once a year—with a message tailored specifically to them. An example of one such message—a letter of proven effectiveness—is shown in Figure 6-8.

Individuals at the lower giving levels who do not respond positively after three or four years of solicitation, should be eliminated from your list. They are a luxury you cannot afford.

Thanks!

This is Your Receipt.

We really mean it. That "we" stands for many people you may never meet but who need and appreciate your financial support . . . people touched by Church education and health service programs worldwide. Because personalized acknowledgment of every gift is prohibitively expensive, we are not always able to send individual letters of appreciation. Consequently, we hope you will accept this communication as a simple but sincere expression of our gratitude.

Account Name:

Account Number:

Date:

Donation Description:

Gifts to charitable institutions are deductible for tax purposes under Sec. 170 of the IRS Code.

Barry B. Preator
Financial Accounting
The Development Office
P.O. Box 7188
University Station
Provo. Utah 84602

Figure 6-1. Combined "Thank You" and Receipt Form

BRIGHAM YOUNG UNIVERSITY

The
W.W. Clyde
Engineering Sciences
and Technology
Building

A SPECIAL HERITAGE IN ENGINEERING AND TECHNOLOGY

Figure 6-2.   Commemorative Brochure—Representative Cover

Mr. Clyde's devotion to Scouting is reflected in the many improvements he made at the Maple Dell Scout Camp in Payson, which included this modern lodge.

Section of interstate near Salt Lake City under construction.

affairs, Mr. Clyde served as mayor of Springville; member, University of Utah Board of Regents and Utah Valley Industrial Development Association; and president, Associated General Contractors, Springville Chamber of Commerce, Springville Kiwanis Club, Springville Art Association, and Timpanogos Knife and Fork Club.

Long a leader in the Boy Scouts of America, he was president of the Utah National Parks Council for twelve years and held the Silver Beaver and Silver Antelope awards. While he was president,

the Scout Office Building in Provo was constructed and the following improvements were made at Maple Dell Scout Camp: swimming pool, amphitheater, and facilities for caretakers and Scout leaders. In addition, Mr. & Mrs. Clyde contributed a modern lodge to the camp.

He served as bishop of the Springville LDS Ninth Ward and as a member of the Springville Stake High Council.

Mr. Clyde's life of distinguished service and contributions was recognized with numerous awards: The BYU Jesse Knight

Figure 6-3.   Commemorative Brochures—Representative Page Layout

*H*e that can heroically endure
adversity will bear prosper-
ity with equal greatness of soul;
for the mind that cannot
be dejected by the former is not likely
to be transported with the latter.
— Henry Fielding
    English novelist

To an extraordinary degree, Dr. and
Mrs. Harold Merkley are Fielding's kind
of people.

Adversity? They have known it —
from the arduous, debt-ridden struggle
through undergraduate and medical
school, to the day-and-night toil of one-
man doctoring in an isolated mining
county of 5,000, to the bone-wearying
work of starting a practice from scratch.

In the summer of 1914, Roland Rich
Woolley, then twenty-three, borrowed
$100 from a former missionary companion
so he could travel to Washington, D. C.,
find a job, and enroll in law school.
That loan launched Mr. Woolley on a
distinguished legal career — a fact he
hasn't forgotten. On April 13, 1973
he gave Brigham Young University
$500,000 to establish a loan fund at the
J. Reuben Clark Law School.

INSTITUTE

Years from now, October 12, 1976 will be
looked upon as an important date not only in
the history of this institution, but in the history
of business in American higher education.

It will be remembered as the beginning of the
Skaggs Institute of Retail Management at
Brigham Young University, established with a
generous grant from the Skaggs Foundation.

Those who look back will see that the institute's
inception signalled the start of a unique and
nationally known organization — one
expressly designed to provide academic *and*
practical retailing education.

Proud statements? Perhaps. But people close
to the institute believe in them. The
information that follows — about the institute
proper and the company that founded it —
helps to reveal why.

Mr. & Mrs. Clyde have made substantial
philanthropic gifts to educational, scientific,
religious, and cultural institutions, including
Brigham Young University, the University of
Utah, Utah State University, and — as
mentioned earlier — the Boy Scouts of
America.

In addition, through the Clyde Foundation
(founded in 1962), Mr. & Mrs. Clyde were
instrumental in the construction of the Clyde
Memorial Galleries for the Springville Art
Museum. The two-story wing, completed in
1964, is named in memory of Mr. Clyde's
parents.

Figure 6-4.   Commemorative Brochures—Representative Paragraphs

Castledale College
Wendover, Utah 84083

Mr. L. W. Bird
1229 Antelope Circle
Lincoln, Nebraska 68506

Dear Mr. Bird:

The events of the past week have been a source of great
satisfaction to all of us here at the College.

We were delighted to have you and Mrs. Bird as our guests
at dinner Friday evening. It was a special pleasure for us
to meet your many friends, including Senator and Mrs. Hill.

Many people have commented about your generosity and
thoughtfulness in establishing the scholarship fund. Mayor
Hawkins told me he could think of no finer gift to the young
people of our community, and Mr. Lambert said the fund was
"one of the best ideas anyone has had to help our community
in many, many years."

May I take this opportunity to thank you again, Mr. Bird,
for your contribution to our institution and its young
people.

We will, of course, provide you with a semi-annual report
on the fund. We will also arrange for you to meet with
students who will be benefitting from the fund. Quarterly
luncheons are planned for this purpose. If we can be of
service in some other way, please call on us.

Sincerely,

Brandon R. Ralphs

Brandon R. Ralphs, President

Figure 6-5. Letter to be Sent Following Thank-You Event

DONOR CULTIVATION DATA CARD   Name _____   Age ____ Date ____

Address _____   City _____ State ____ Zip ____ Phone (___) ____

Birth Date _____   Spouse's Name/Birth Date ____

Children's Names _____

Donor's Occupation _____   Giving History (gifts, value, when given) ____

Names of Close Friends/Business Associates ____

Interests/Hobbies/Accomplishments ____

List key factors that led donor to give to our organization ____

_____   Religion ____   Political Pref. ____

Is Donor Favorable Toward Publicity? ____   Special Qualities, Needs, Problems

Relating to Donor ____

Describe here and on backside specific cultivation plan for future gifts, includ-

ing publications, invitations to be extended, etc. ____

Figure 6-6.   Donor Cultivation Data Card

The Development Office   **Brigham Young University**

Dear Friend of BYU:

Year in and year out you've been somebody we could
count on--a steady supporter of Brigham Young University. If we haven't said so lately, let us say so
now: we appreciate you!

My reason for writing is to ask your help in making
our Annual Giving program as efficient as possible.
Let me explain.

As you know, each year we depend on hundreds of
volunteer workers to make personal contacts on behalf of BYU. If we could persuade you and the many
others who contribute to BYU to make your contribution automatic, it would free our workers to zero
in on those who have not yet demonstrated the
loyalty you have.

What we propose to do is to simply remind you each
year (via a computerized statement) of the need for
your gift to BYU. The date the statement is mailed
and the amount to be given are, of course, up to you.
We call our program Auto Giving.

We hope we aren't being presumptuous, and we hope
you can appreciate the time and money-saving advantages of an automatic statement program.

To initiate Auto Giving, fill in the enclosed
card and return it in the pre-addressed envelope.

Thanks!

Sincerely,

Ken "J" Taylor, Assistant Director

P. S. Please respond by July 1.

University Station, P.O. Box 7188, Brigham Young University, Provo, Utah 84602
(801) 374-1211, Extension 4444

**Figure 6-7.   Letter to Loyal Givers Announcing Streamlined Solicitation
Approach**

Dallin H. Oaks
President

Brigham Young University

Talk to alumni who haven't contributed to BYU in the past
and you'll hear comments like this:

"I haven't given because, well, I haven't felt the University
really needed my money."

I want you to know that Brigham Young University <u>does</u> need
your financial support, and that your gift--large or small--
is welcomed and wanted.

We have innumerable needs as we begin our second century
of educational service--needs involving scholarships, loan
funds, research, endowed professorial chairs, and much more.

Many individuals--parents, friends, alumni--who have not
given to BYU in the past, have taken the opportunity to do
so in this first year of our second century.

I hope you will do the same.

Sincerely,

Dallin H. Oaks

D-346 ASB, Brigham Young University, Provo, Utah 84602 (801) 374-1211, Extension 2521

Figure 6-8.   Letter to Non-Givers

Chapter Seven

HOW IT HAPPENS: THREE CASE HISTORIES

If fund-raisers kept diaries (some do), and if they were given to writing fiction (some are), a typical entry might read as follows:

Dear Diary: What an incredible day! Just as I sat down at my desk this morning, Mr. B. J. Glassman called me. Yep, that's right —*the* Mr. Glassman. Imagine—*him* calling me . . . called all the way from Monaco. Oh, we had jokingly brought up his name a few times in our Prospect Consideration Meetings—along with those of Nelson Rockefeller, Bob Hope and Walter Cronkite! But you know, he acted like he was my long-lost friend. Said he knew all about Oakville Hospital and our plans to add a 100-bed wing and the new emergency center. Said he thought it was the right thing to do, and—can you believe it?—said he wanted to help! Next thing I know he's asking me how much the whole thing will cost. I managed to mumble, 'Ah, ah, about $4 million, Mr. Glass-man—that's with the automatic doors on the emergency center and all.' Then he said, 'Well, sir, would a million in a day or two and a million each month for the next three months be OK? I mean cash, of course.' I'm almost choking by now, but I worry about sounding too eager (and besides that, I'm wondering if someone is playing a practical joke on me), so I come back with, 'Well . . . hmmmm . . . we could probably accept that—yes, yes, I believe that would work out, Mr. Glassman. Ya, I definitely feel that it would . . . I think I have authority to say that.' Then he said, 'Fine, good, wonderful. I was hoping you would feel that way. Let's see now, what is the hospital's full legal name—so I get it on the checks correctly. Also, I need your Zip code out there. . . .'

The foregoing is, of course, the wildest kind of fantasy. Anyone who has been raising funds for even a week knows that the chances of something like that happening are too remote to calculate. True, you do get some pleasant surprises every once in a while—a $100 bill in the mail from an anonymous donor with a note reading "keep up the great work"; an honest-in-heart prospect who comes knocking on *your* door; an envelope from a law firm containing notice of a $5,000 bequest to your organization. But almost without exception, truly substantial gifts involve months, sometimes years of painstaking planning, cultivation and even negotiation. In short, most big gifts "happen" because able and ambitious fund-raisers *make* them happen.

The paragraphs that follow present three case histories of large gifts actually received by charitable organizations from individual donors. These histories are recommended reading because they dramatize the application of fund-raising principles that *work*. They have worked in the past for others and will work in the future for you. As you read the histories, look for evidence that the fund-raisers have tried to:

○ Establish a functional, efficient organization in which each worker's duties are clearly defined.
○ Establish a just cause and effectively communicate it.
○ Identify individuals who could reasonably be expected to contribute, and carefully evaluate their giving interests and potential.
○ Cultivate prospects by honestly earning their friendship and trust.
○ Apply, where appropriate, those factors that motivate people to give.
○ Demonstrate personal commitment to their causes.

o Use existing facilities, services, special circumstances and personnel (including volunteers) with maximum effectiveness.
o Involve appropriate people in cultivational and asking activities.
o Understand and capitalize on the *prospect's* value system, priorities and frame of reference.
o Persevere, whatever the difficulties and setbacks.
o Make effective and optimum use of solicitation techniques and tools.
o Involve professionals when appropriate.
o Apply pressure to overcome prospect inertia.
o Tailor their requests to their prospects.
o Comply with ethical, professional standards of conduct.

So that the author could write freely about the events that took place, the names of the people involved in each case history are fictitious and the receiving organizations are not specifically identified.

CASE HISTORY A

Mrs. Brown, a wealthy, 63-year-old widow living in Nevada, read a wire service story describing encouraging progress a university speech researcher in California was making in treating stammering. Mrs. Brown's late husband had struggled with the handicap for years, and had made only marginal progress in overcoming it.

The story had been written by the university news director at the urging of Mr. Johnson, the university development director. The story contained a quote by the researcher, Dr. Glenn, in which he said, "With additional funding support, we can continue to make important progress in helping people with this difficult problem."

A few days after she had read the article, Brown reached Glenn by phone at the university and asked several questions about his work. He was alert enough to sense that she was seriously interested in his research and a possible source of financial support. Glenn was courteous, helpful and patient. He told Brown he would like to send her some articles he had published, and asked for her name and address. She complied.

Glenn mailed the material to Brown three days later, together with a warm, friendly cover letter. About two weeks after that, he received a simple thank-you note from Brown. Glenn then went to Johnson (the development director) and told him about Brown. Johnson asked Glenn to inform him of any future calls or letters from Brown, and then asked his research supervisor (Mrs. Henderson) to find out all she could about Brown and to give him a report.

Henderson called an alumnus, Mr. Phillips, who lived in Brown's city. Phillips was an attorney who had helped the university in various professional and volunteer capacities. Because Brown's late husband had been a prominent CPA in the city, Phillips quickly was able to gather important information about the couple. Phillips talked to neighbors and former business associates of Mr. Brown, and located his obituary at the city library. Within a month, Henderson had a substantial file on the Browns, including religious preference, political affiliation, value of the estate, past giving patterns and organizational membership.

Although Glenn had heard nothing further from Brown, Johnson decided—on the basis of Henderson's encouraging findings—to initiate a cultivation program. He asked Glenn to begin sending Brown informative, nontechnical materials relating to speech therapy and communicative disorders. Each mailing was to be accompanied by a friendly, low-key, "thought you might be interested" cover letter signed by Glenn. Each cover letter was to include an invitation to call or write for additional information. Johnson asked his communications supervisor to help Glenn prepare the mailings.

After two mailings had been made (about one month's time), Johnson called Phillips (the volunteer-attorney) and asked him to invite Brown and a companion to a play to be put on by the university's traveling drama group in Brown's city. Phillips was to explain that he was a friend of the university and of Glenn, and that he had been asked by Glenn to invite her to the play. Brown accepted, and decided to attend the play with her daughter. Phillips picked them up at their home, took them to the play and then to dinner.

Over dessert, Phillips *carefully* talked about the university, Glenn's work, and the fact that people can sometimes help worthy causes—and themselves—through proper estate planning. He suggested that Brown consider visiting the university and seeing at first hand the work of Glenn. Brown was polite and attentive but noncommittal.

About a week later, Glenn called Brown and invited her to be the university's guest for three days. Her visit would include a tour of Glenn's department, a visit with the university president and a front-row seat at a concert. Brown declined the offer. She gave no reason.

Glenn continued to send materials to her. In addition, Phillips began sending her commercially prepared pamphlets about the importance of wills and estate planning.

Several months passed. Glenn was preparing a regional-level workshop for speech therapists. Leading authorities from several states would be in attendance, and important papers would be presented. He decided that the workshop was an ideal excuse to invite Brown again to the campus. Glenn wrote her a letter describing the workshop and inviting her to be the university's guest. He followed up the letter with a telephone call about a week later. This time Brown accepted the invitation.

Johnson, his staff and Glenn worked together to make certain that Brown's visit was a *total* success. Some specifics:

○ They met her at the airport and drove her to her hotel—one of the city's best.

○ In her room, she found a basket of fruit with a card inscribed, "We hope your visit is enjoyable and memorable. Please call if there's anything you need. Dr. Glenn and _____ University."

○ They arranged for her to meet the university president, tour the campus (via electric golf cart), talk with students and patients in the speech therapy department and visit several points of interest in the city and surrounding area. The president gave her an inscribed copy of a book he had just published.

○ They *sincerely* sought her comments and suggestions about higher education in general and about speech problems in particular.

○ When it was time for her to leave, they dropped by the president's office. He thanked her for coming and wished her an enjoyable trip home. Then they drove her to the airport.

A few days after her departure, Glenn sent a brief note thanking her for her visit. Included with the note were copies of some of the papers presented at the workshop.

About two weeks later, Phillips called Brown and told her that he and Glenn would like to meet with her in her home to discuss some ways in which she could further Glenn's work and possibly strengthen her financial position. Brown agreed to meet them.

Before Phillips and Glenn visited Brown and asked for the gift, Phillips determined how much to ask for and what form the gift should take. These decisions were based on the best available information about Brown's assets.

Outcome: Brown decided to place her $300,000 estate in a short-term trust with the university, restricted to Glenn's department. Upon her death, the university will receive annually 6 percent of the initial value of the trust for 10 years. After this period, the trust will end and the daughter will own the property. This arrangement will largely eliminate the estate tax on Brown's estate.

CASE HISTORY B

A private, church-sponsored college in the Midwest had been cultivating the 60-ish owner of a chain of restaurants (Mr. Hart) for about two years. Mr. Hart, a faithful member of the church that sponsored the college, had been very successful. For years he had pursued a rich man's hobby: collecting prize-winning big-game trophies he personally shot on hunting trips worldwide. His collection contained over 75 trophies, including a Bengal tiger, Cape buffalo and kongoni antelope.

Mr. Redd, the college's fund-raising director, was, of course, aware of Hart's wealth. He was, however, only vaguely aware of his love of big-game hunting and of his trophy collection.

One day Dr. Jensen, curator of the college's life sciences collection, visited Redd and told him about Hart's big-game collection. (Jensen had only recently learned of the collection from a colleague.) Jensen suggested that perhaps Hart would consider giving the collection to the college. His reasoning was that the collection required a great deal of space in the Hart home, that Hart and his wife were getting on in years and that the college would give the collection excellent care and expose it to thousands of people.

Redd had some reservations about Jensen's idea. First, he wasn't sure the college really wanted a collection of big-game trophies. And second, he was concerned about where the college would house the collection. "We really don't have a place that would do justice to something like that . . . we'd probably have to build something somewhere," he told Jensen.

Redd was, however, grateful for Jensen's visit, because it suggested a specific direction for future cultivational activities. Redd asked Jensen to begin sending Hart cultivational materials, including a newsletter, a series of articles about African big game, and a research paper on Alaskan wildlife. He urged Jensen to try to meet Hart and to earn his friendship and trust.

For years Jensen had dreamed of a comprehensive, self-contained life sciences museum for the campus. Such a museum would facilitate research and make his excellent collections—everything from birds' eggs to beetles—readily accessible to researchers, students and the public. (As things were, his collections were scattered in three different buildings, inadequately stored and protected and not readily available for educational and research purposes.) Jensen saw in the Hart situation an opportunity to get the big-game trophies *and* his life sciences museum. His plan: sell Hart on the idea of giving the college the trophies *and* of building a museum to house them.

Jensen set about in earnest to cultivate Hart. He sent the previously described materials with a cover letter in which he introduced himself and asked if he could visit Hart and see the collection. He said he would call Hart in a few days. About a week later, Jensen called Hart and reiterated his desire to see the collection. Hart was agreeable, and a week later Jensen was in Hart's home as his guest for two days. Before he left to visit Hart, however, Jensen learned everything he could about the man, including politics, hobbies and interests besides hunting, and the locations of all of his restaurants.

Within about three months, Jensen and Hart had become

good friends. Each respected the knowledge and accomplishments of the other. Jensen, who had a doctorate in zoology, gave Hart some stimulating scientific insights into big game. Hart, on the other hand, enjoyed the attention Jensen gave him and the opportunity to associate with a respected member of academia. (Hart had never attended college.)

About six weeks after Jensen's visit to the Hart home, Jensen succeeded in having Hart visit the campus as his guest. He introduced him to the college president, to his colleagues and to Redd. He devoted two full days to showing him his marvelous collections. During this time, Jensen took Hart into his confidence. He told him of his dream to build a life sciences museum where the college's collections could be adequately, impressively displayed. He talked about the great research and educational value of specimens. And he pointed out that the college was ideally suited for a life sciences museum (there was not a good one in the entire state, and the college had a strong life sciences faculty and curriculum).

At this point, Hart responded almost on cue. He told Jensen he was going to donate his big-game collection to the college. Jensen reacted warmly to the news. He made it clear, however, that he was concerned about whether he should accept the collection in view of the fact that the college did not have a place to properly display it. (Hart had apparently assumed that if he donated his collection, the college would build the museum.) Jensen thanked Hart and told him he would be in touch with him about the matter.

Jensen then went to Redd and informed him of Hart's offer. Jensen asked Redd if he thought the college would be interested in having a life sciences museum if Hart built it. The college, of course, would donate the land and pay operating expenses. Redd felt that the college would be interested. He and Jensen subsequently met with the president and received his approval to make a proposal to Hart using that approach. They also received approval to name the museum the Reed F. Hart Life Sciences Museum.

With the help of the college physical plant department and the communications specialist on Redd's staff, Jensen began to prepare a request to Hart. It contained a site plan, floor plan (including square footage), equipment list, architectural renderings of the proposed museum, benefits of the museum to the college and community and estimated cost. The name "Reed F. Hart Life Sciences Museum" appeared prominently on the building in the renderings.

Jensen and Redd met with Redd's planned-giving specialist (a CPA) to get advice on how Hart could best make the gift from a tax standpoint. Since most of Hart's wealth was in the restaurant stock he held, Jensen planned to suggest that Hart make a gift of appreciated property in the form of the stock.

During the three months the proposal was in preparation, Jensen continued to cultivate Hart. He made it clear that the college was grateful for his offer to donate the collection. He told Hart that a proposal was in preparation that would make it possible for the college to accept the collection and properly house it.

When the proposal was ready, Jensen made an appointment with Hart, and he (Jensen), Redd and the college president met with Hart in his office. Using charts, the proposal proper, and other materials they had prepared, they outlined their plans for the museum. They were careful, however, to explain that they were flexible, and that they wanted and needed Hart's ideas and suggestions. They ended by asking for $2.5 million to build the museum. Hart was warm to the idea, but said he wanted time to consult with his financial advisers and to study it carefully.

Following the presentation, Jensen and the president maintained friendly, low-key contact with Hart. Several months went by with no firm decision from him. About six months after the presentation, Redd offered what proved to be an important suggestion. He noted that the college was about to launch a capital campaign in connection with the 75th anniversary of its founding. He suggested that they tell Hart that the college wanted to announce his gift at the kick-off banquet for the capital campaign. Such an announcement would get the campaign off to an excellent start and would encourage others to contribute. Subsequently, Jensen and the president jointly expressed that desire in a letter to Hart. They told him if he was agreeable, they would honor him and his wife at the banquet.

Outcome: Hart agreed to give the college a total of $2.5 million in stock over five years. And he did, by the way, have some ideas of his own about how the museum should be built!

CASE HISTORY C

Mr. Wright, the fund-raiser for a church-operated boys' home in the southeastern United States, was given a prospect referral by a member of the church. The prospect's name was Mr. Timms. He was a wealthy, 58-year-old inventor living in Kansas. Significantly, Timms had spent his childhood in several foster homes, and both he and his wife were active members of the church that operated the boys' home for which Wright was raising funds.

Although Wright recognized that the home's distance from Timms was a major disadvantage, he felt the other factors made Timms an excellent prospect. His first step was to call the pastor of Timms' church in Kansas. Wright's call netted him two major benefits: (1) Important additional information about Timms, and (2) a pledge from the pastor to help cultivate Timms to contribute to the boys' home. (Fortunately, Timms' local church was not operating a boys' home or any other institution that might have competed for his contribution.)

Wright then wrote a letter to Timms introducing himself and the boys' home. The letter was brief but offered some credible specifics, including the number of boys the home had helped in its 56 years of existence, and some of its needs. Wright also began sending Timms case histories of boys who had "graduated" from the home and had become responsible, contributing members of society.

Wright's cultivation effort was cut short, however, by a call from the pastor. He told Wright that Timms had suffered some financial reverses, and suggested that he stop cultivating him. Wright complied.

Nine years passed. Wright had completely forgotten about Timms. Then, out of the blue, Wright received a call from the pastor. His message: Timms had made a financial recovery and was once again a promising prospect. The pastor sug-

gested that Wright resume cultivational activities, and, as before, he promised to assist.

Wright wrote Timms a second letter reintroducing himself
and the boys' home. Again, he told Timms of the home's
solid, documented accomplishments in helping young men.
This time, however, Wright was able to add that the home
was in the midst of a capital campaign to raise $500,000 to
build a new, greatly expanded facility with a swimming pool,
tennis courts, shop, gymnasium and library. Wright was careful not to ask Timms for a contribution. He simply informed
him of the home's activities and aspirations, and said that he
would send along additional information from time to time.
Wright realized that asking for the gift at this point—especially by mail—would have probably resulted in a token,
"buy off" gift. Obviously, he didn't want that to happen.

About this time something happened that made Wright feel
that God did, indeed, want the boys to have a new home: The
home's baseball team won its regional playoff and qualified
to play for the national championship. Playing site: Kansas
City, Kansas—20 miles from Mr. Timms' residence.

Wright quickly realized that the baseball team's trip to
Kansas City offered some tremendous cultivational opportunities. It would, of course, give him a chance to meet Timms
personally, talk to him about the boys' home and the campaign, "read" his reactions and then tailor an approach to him
for later presentation. But in addition, it would enable Wright
to bring to bear some important, supplemental strategy
involving:

○ Arranging for Timms and his wife to be the home's guests at one
   of the ball games, sit with the national head of the church and
   meet the ball players.
○ Taking Timms and his wife to dinner where they would meet the
   founder and president of the boys' home and 10 "graduates"—all
   successful, established citizens. Each would give a brief, hope-
   fully inspirational talk about how he felt about the boys' home.
   (Because of his age—95—and poor health, the boys' home president would not be attending any of the ball games.)
○ Meeting with close friends and business associates of Timms
   who could help fill in some financial details. (Wright wasn't sure,
   for example, what form Timms' contribution should take. With

additional information, he could ask an attorney to develop the best tax-planned giving approach.)

Ideally, Wright needed more time to cultivate Timms via mail and phone calls. The playoffs, however, were only two weeks away. He called the pastor, explained the situation and asked his advice. The pastor recommended that Wright call Timms and invite him and his wife to the functions. The pastor said that he would prepare Timms for the call and do what he could to encourage a positive response.

After giving the pastor time to do his part, Wright called Timms and extended the ball-game and dinner invitations. Wright, wisely, was not coy with Timms. He told him that representatives of the home wanted to meet with him at some later date—after the Kansas meetings—to acquaint him further with the boys' home and some of its specific needs. (He had in mind inviting Timms and his wife to the home as special guests, but did not mention this on the phone.) Timms accepted the invitations.

After extensive work, and with the help of a volunteer who lived in Kansas City and the pastor, Wright completed all the arrangements. Once in Kansas City, he made an all-out effort to give the Timmses the red-carpet treatment. He and the pastor picked them up at their home, took a sincere interest in them, and extended them every proper courtesy. During the dinner, Wright learned that Mrs. Timms was interested in genealogy, and that she was attempting to trace her father's forebears whom she believed had lived in Virginia. He made a mental note to send her a newly available computerized list of everyone with the Green surname (her maiden name) who had lived in Virginia when federal censuses had been taken. Before the dinner was over, Wright had invited the Timmses to be his guests at the boys' home a month later. They accepted.

Between the Kansas City events and the Timmses visit to the boys' home, Wright wrote two letters to them. The first was a warm thank-you note for the opportunity to meet with them and enjoy their company. The second was a letter reminding them of their pending visit and asking for specific arrival time, including airline and flight number. This letter included a postscript reading: "Mrs. Timms—You should receive shortly under separate cover a computerized list of all Greens who lived in Virginia during the 1800's. I hope this helps you trace your father's ancestors."

With the help of a professional, freelance writer, Wright put together a presentation package that incorporated all the elements he felt would have maximum appeal to Timms. During his Kansas City visit, for example, he had learned that Timms was work-ethic oriented—that he felt contemporary young people needed to be taught how to work. Consequently, his proposal made specific mention of the fact that every boy in the home had a rotating schedule of chores to do six days a week.

The package also included a suggested way for Timms to make the gift based on what Wright had been able to learn in Kansas City about his financial situation. The suggested approach, prepared with an attorney's help, reflected estate planning and tax considerations.

When the Timmses arrived in Wright's city, he essentially repeated his Kansas City red-carpet treatment. He met them at the airport, took them to the home where they received a tour and met each boy, took them to dinner and then to their hotel. He told them that the national church leader they had met in Kansas City would be with them for lunch the next day, and that he would pick them up at 11:30.

Wright made the presentation at the lunch, but the church leader added some words of endorsement and support. The presentation included the suggestion that the new facility be named the "Stanley & Alice Timms Center." The attorney who had helped Wright prepare the presentation was at the luncheon and answered several questions that Timms asked.

Outcome: Timms placed appreciated securities worth $400,000 in an annuity trust for himself, his wife and the boys' home. He and his wife receive annuity payments that increase their spendable income. In addition, they receive a charitable income-tax deduction and much of their trust will avoid taxation when Mr. Timms dies. Mrs. Timms will receive annuity payments for however long she survives her husband. When she dies, the trust will end and the remaining assets will go to the boys' home.

Chapter Eight

"WHY I GAVE":
TWELVE DONORS TALK

$\mathbf{I}$f you can discover why people give, you can improve your fund-raising effectiveness. It is for this reason that the psychology of giving is analyzed in detail in Chapter 2. In a sense, this chapter is a continuation of Chapter 2, except that *donors* do the talking. In *their* words, they tell why they gave.

The author interviewed 12 donors who had contributed varying amounts in several different ways to a range of charitable organizations. To encourage frank responses, the donors were told that their comments would be kept confidential and published anonymously. Nevertheless, some of the donors' responses are probably less than candid, but even so, it is helpful to hear what donors *say* are the reasons why they gave, because if the donors are comfortable and secure with these reasons, then the latter merit our attention on that basis alone.

In fund-raising, as in politics, medicine, law and many other disciplines, there are "code" words and phrases exquisitely engineered to (a) conceal rather than reveal, (b) sound good and be socially/professionally acceptable, and (c) discourage further probing. Here are some examples of "code" words and phrases typically used by donors (watch for variations of these in the 12 donor statements on the pages that follow):

"We gave because we believe in the college and its educational program." (*Comment:* This may be true, but it probably wasn't *the* motivating force. Recognition, acceptance, tax benefits and the other factors described in Chapter 2 are far more credible explanations.)

"I agreed to publicity only so that others would know of my gift and be encouraged to make similar gifts." (*Comment:* Doubtful. This donor, typical of many donors, suggested that a photograph of him and the institutional president accompany the news release. In addition, he supplied a two-page biography and asked to receive all newspaper clippings. If his sole purpose in authorizing publicity was to promote the receiving organization, why didn't he ask that the news release omit his name and simply refer to him as an "anonymous donor"? This approach would have accomplished his expressed purpose of stimulating others to give. Obviously, this donor likes recognition but doesn't want to admit it.)

"I gave because I thought it was the right and proper thing to do." (*Comment:* Acceptable as a *partial* explanation. Unless the gift is a very small one, there's more to the story, and it can be found in one or more of the seven factors described in Chapter 2.)

"This contribution is our way of saying thanks for all the Center has done for our child." (*Comment:* Again, acceptable only as a *partial* explanation. It's likely that one of the chief factors that motivated the gift was a desire on the part of the parents to ensure that the Center would *continue* to help their child. This is a variation of the self-preservation element described in Chapter 2).

* * *

Donor 1 (aged 36, land-developer):   Gave his alma mater (a large, private university) controlling interest in a section of valuable coal-bearing land in Colorado. He restricted the gift to the College of Business. Potential value: into the tens of millions.

"I had a long-standing desire to help the university and the College of Business in particular. I owe much of my success to the preparation and insights my business professors gave me . . . I wanted to do something to pay them back. I think that my gift will make their business program even stronger. I would like to see them achieve national prominence. Tax considerations certainly made it easier and more attractive for me to give, and *were* a factor. Also, I like recognition . . . have a deep-seated need for it. I was pleased when the university asked about publicity and—with my approval—took photographs, wrote a news story and released them to the media."

Donor 2 (aged 41, general contractor):   Executed a will arranging for a major portion of his estate to pass to his alma mater (a junior college on the West Coast). His estate was valued at $4 million when the will was executed.

"I felt the college's church sponsor would advance the spiritual ideals on which I had based my life, and which had made me successful. The college has a strict program of spiritual training and high standards for faculty and students—I want to perpetuate these qualities . . . feel they are sadly lacking in contemporary America. I do not want all of my wealth to pass to my children. I think unearned wealth can destroy initiative . . . want my kids to work for what they get. I agreed to publicity for one reason: in the hope that my example will encourage others to make similar gifts to the college."

Donor 3 (aged 50, sports store owner in the Northwest): Gave a fully equipped motor boat and three canoes to a parochial high school for use in a water sports course. Approximate value: $6,500.

"I'm basically stingy about donating, except where the church is concerned. I believe in their programs—both secular and ecclesiastical. I know that when I contribute to the church, they will use my money well. I am convinced that the teachers at the high school are dedicated, competent and work hard for our young people. Recognition—a big article in the newspaper—is not important to me. I think it's counter to the Christian spirit of giving. And I don't think giving is necessarily good for my business. One of my customers who heard about my contribution said something like this to me: 'Well, if you can afford to give so much away, you probably don't need *my* business.' Another reason I gave is because I would rather control where my money goes than simply turn it over to the Internal Revenue Service. Our taxes breed the one thing we don't need more of—bureaucracy. And as far as I'm concerned, bureaucracy means more big government, big waste and wild-eyed social programs that take away people's incentive to work."

Donor 4 (aged 64, Florida gynecologist): Established a unitrust for herself and the hospital with which she was affiliated for much of her professional life. She transferred to the hospital in trust $60,000 worth of securities. Each year the value of the trust assets are determined by the trustees, and the donor receives 5 percent.

"I had a threefold motivation—I wanted some tax relief, wanted to contribute to the hospital and wanted to assure myself of continuing spendable income. Tax relief took the form of a charitable contribution deduction on my income tax, avoidance of capital gains tax and some estate tax benefits when I die. The hospital will receive the value of the trust assets when I'm gone. I have long felt obligated to the hospital: It was the source of my livelihood and the place where I built my professional reputation. I want to be well thought of by my associates, patients and others . . . want to be remembered in a positive way. I believe the hospital is a good one. I want to see it maintain its excellence, and perhaps do more in research. Also, I felt some pressure to give: Many of my associates have given comparable gifts."

Donor 5 (aged 27, Chicago sheet metal worker): Pledged $20 to a policeman's benefit association in response to a telephone solicitation.

"It's hard for me to say no when someone wants my help . . . when they come right out and ask me. I want people to like me. I feel that I have failed or fallen short in some way when I refuse to help people. I'd rather pay the $20 than feel bad about it for several days because I didn't pay it. Twenty dollars isn't very much . . . I can handle that much. I think the police here work hard and deserve a little help. They have a tough job, really, and they earn every bit of what they get. Besides, the person who called was a woman with a *great* voice. I couldn't say no to that!"

Donor 6 (aged 46, owner of a fast-food restaurant near a Utah college campus):   Gave the college $500 cash (unrestricted) and pledged an additional $500 each year for five years. He was awarded membership in the college's President's Club for his contribution and received a plaque. He displays the plaque in a prominent place in his restaurant.

"I give for different reasons at different times. In this case, I gave mainly because I feel that I owe the college something. Most of my customers are students at the college, and they have been good to me . . . made me successful. I wanted to return the favor—do something to help their institution. So it was, I guess, a 'business decision.' I might add, though, that I believe in the college,. I think it is a good influence in the community. I'm comfortable giving them my money. I would say that tax considerations are a subordinate factor in my giving. Tax breaks encourage me to give—reinforce my tendency to give, but they are not the primary factor."

Donor 7 (aged 61, college botany professor in New England):   Gave his college an outright gift of an apartment house valued at $200,000. He stipulated that the college sell the apartment house and use the proceeds to establish a scholarship fund for nursing students. The fund carries the name of his mother. Interest earned on the principal provides full tuition and fees for eight nursing students each year.

"My mother was a nurse—a noble, wonderful, dedicated nurse. She worked very hard, and also served as a midwife. I wanted to honor her memory and to help financially young women interested in nursing careers. I was comfortable giving to the nursing program for another reason: The dean there enjoys a lot of autonomy—isn't all wrapped up in administrative politics, paperwork and red tape. I knew that my money would be used efficiently and for the use I intended. Tax factors didn't make me decide to give—they just made it easier for me to do so. I asked for some publicity . . . felt I deserved it. Also, I hoped the publicity would stimulate gifts for the college from others."

Donor 8 (aged 52, owner of a medium-sized grocery store in the Midwest):   Gave $2,500 in cash to a boys' club to help them build a new club house.

"My brother says I've always given everything away . . . been too free with my belongings. He says I've always gone overboard. I don't know. I guess I feel bad for those kids whose parents have sort of copped out on them. When the boys' club president and two of the boys visited me and asked for the money, I just didn't want to refuse. I felt good that they would think of me in that way—as somebody who would be willing to help . . . do a good thing like that. They made me feel important, and I just couldn't let them down. Giving to them really gave me a lift—joy, I guess, is the word. You know, after you make some big purchase—new car, boat, something like that—you feel blue about it for days afterward, wondering if you did the right thing. But after I gave that $2,500, it wasn't that way. It was just a great feeling, and the feeling comes back every time I think about it."

Donor 9 (aged 48, Pennsylvania home-builder):   Gave $25,000 cash over a three-year period to help finance an addition to a local hospital.

"That hospital is part of me and my family . . . reaches back to my grandparents. I was born there, my grandfather and father died there. My kids have been born there. The hospital has always been there when we needed it. It seemed funny for the hospital, all of a sudden, to need me. The people who asked me to give—the director and one of the doctors—were right out with it. They said they needed $25,000 from successful members of the community and would I give. In a tactful way they pointed out what the hospital had given me and would continue to give me and my family in the future. They said the expansion would result in better facilities, better health care. I was wavering a bit. Then they talked about some tax advantages, and showed me how my gift would affect my taxes (they had really scouted me!). After I consulted with my own attorney, which they encouraged me to do, I decided to give. Boiled down, it was a matter of discharging an obligation I felt to the hospital in a way that wasn't too painful. Part of it, too, was the fact that I was helping people in the community who had given me my livelihood by buying houses from me."

Donor 10 (aged 67, housewife and widow):   Gave $11,200 cash to improve agriculture on an American Indian reservation in Arizona.

"My late husband and I worked with the Indian people throughout the Southwest for many years. He was with a governmental Indian agency, and I took an active interest in his work. We both came to respect and love the Indian people. He and I never talked about it openly, but I think we both felt guilty about our family having so much more than the Indians—materially, I mean. I decided that I wanted to do *something* to help them. Agriculture seemed like a sensible philanthropic investment . . . something that would literally reap dividends. The disability and mortality rates of American Indians are still shamefully high. With good agriculture, however, they can improve their health and perhaps develop another source of income to improve their standard of living."

Donor 11 (aged 44, prominent California dentist):   Gave $15,000 cash to a university special-gift club devoted to athletics. His contribution entitled him to lifetime membership in the club and to several worthwhile benefits, including VIP treatment for parking and tickets.

"I was going to lose the money anyway—if not to the athletic club, then to Uncle Sam. By giving to the club, I had some say about where my money went, and I got some privileges that I enjoy and—frankly—that are good for my professional image. This is probably going to sound bad, but you asked me to be honest: You see, it's important for professional people to have the accoutrements of success . . . yes, even to be seen sitting in good seats at a basketball game! I recognize that. It's a lot like life insurance salesmen driving Cadillacs . . . good for business. I don't think, though, that my contribution was without charitable intent. I was pleased to be able to help promote the university through athletics. After all, I did my undergraduate work at that school. They are the people who got me started."

Donor 12 (aged 63, New York television executive): Placed his $600,000 estate in unitrust for his wife and their church. This arrangement involves two trusts, and takes advantage of both marital and charitable deductions. It will eliminate federal estate tax on the executive's estate when he dies, and may well eliminate estate tax on his wife's estate upon her death. When she dies, the principal of one of the trusts will go as her will directs; the principal of the other trust will go to their church.

"We didn't set out to give money to our church. Rather, my wife and I went to our attorney for some estate-planning help. It was he who made us aware of the fact that we could conserve our estate and help our church at the same time. I was aware of the fact that the church was looking to me for some financial help, but my first concern was to take care of my wife and our children. When it became clear that helping the church was in some ways supportive of what I wanted to do for my wife and family—well, that clinched it. I've thought about other aspects of why I gave, and I've really tried to analyze it honestly. Maybe this isn't profound, but it seems to me that when people get into their 60's or so, they feel the world is leaving them behind—which, of course, it is. They feel their influence and power ebbing, especially if they've had some influence and power in their younger years. So it seems to me that giving in one's sunset years is one way to have some impact—wield some power, if you will —when physically, mentally and position-wise you're beginning to *lose* power. Maybe giving is a way to strike back in your declining years . . . maybe a way to soften the swing of the grim reaper."

Chapter Nine

ADVICE FROM VETERANS

. . . men are my teachers.
—PLATO

Fund-raisers would do well to adapt Plato's statement to read, "Other fund-raisers are my teachers." The point is, of course, that fund-raising takes in so much territory and encompasses so many skills that no one person's experience can ever be enough.

With that in mind, the author turned to respected, established fund-raisers across the country for their ideas about the art of asking. Specifically, they were asked to respond to this question: "If you had only a few minutes to counsel someone about fund-raising—a person with little to moderate fund-raising experience—what would you tell him or her?"

Their responses, which follow, were warmly and graciously given, and reflected a sincere desire to be helpful. What they had to say covers a remarkable range of concerns and provides convincing evidence that fund-raising is, indeed, an eclectic, diverse discipline.

* * *

"I am constantly amazed at the number of significant institutions and organizations who plan and implement fund-

raising programs without consideration for, or even understanding of, what I consider to be the entire essence of
the profession—marketing!

"Fund-raising is but the nonprofit world's equivalent of
selling, except instead of a physical product to be offered in
the marketplace, the offering is of an idea or concept. American business has very sharply refined the process of marketing, with little doubt left as to probable results after proper
consumer research is undertaken, good sales strategy established, effective advertising and promotion initiated and the
sales force trained and provided with necessary aids.

"Most nonprofit groups would benefit by emulating the
marketing practices of business and industry. It is totally er-
roneous to assume that because a charity is a good one and
meets a community need it will be supported. In twenty
years of fund-raising (during which I have raised over $38
million for clients) I have seen this ' I deserve support and
therefore will get it ' attitude over and over again. But successful programs must be built on a solid base of understanding the prospect (research), developing the right cultivation
process (advertising), and effectively evoking support
(sales)."

> —HOWARD M. SCHWARTZ
> President
> Howard M. Schwartz & Associates, Inc.
> Philadelphia, Pennsylvania

*   *   *

"It's relatively easy to raise monies for something that's
tangible. Few schools have real difficulty in getting alumni,
parents and friends to make contributions toward the construction of a new gym or fine arts center where they can en-
vision results. However, most schools which are not extraor-
dinarily endowed are forced to conduct annual fund-raising
drives to help pay for *operating expenses*. The term has no
glamorous ring to it; consequently, it is the hardest expense
to meet, and yet it is vital. It challenges one to come up with
the most innovative ideas and determined action.

"Building a case for meeting this annual demand is one of the development director's most difficult tasks. A way of tackling this problem is to ensure that your school is indeed worthy of being maintained. Is the school as good as you say it is? If your image isn't good, people will be reluctant to help you make up any deficit in your operations. On the other hand, if you have a salable product with strong traditions and quality education, stress this theme in all your appeals for dollars. Congratulate your parents, for example, on their wisdom in choosing your school over its competition—compliment their good judgement. Then, make it clear to them and to your other constituencies that without extra gifts over and above tuition and other regular sources of income, you simply will not be able to continue to maintain those extra advantages offered by your school which make it stronger than other schools. Increased tuition beyond a certain point is not the answer.

"To sum up, remind your givers that every school cost from heating buildings to maintaining the campus to teachers' salaries increases annually in these inflationary times. In order to balance the budget and not sacrifice those extras that make your school stand out, extra giving must be expected and realized."

—JAMES S. GARDNER
Director of Development
Park-Tudor School
Indianapolis, Indiana

*   *   *

"A number of years ago I chose fund-raising as a thesis subject for my graduate degree in business management. The results of that research taught me a fund-raising fundamental that has served me well through the years.

"The factors that most closely correlated with the success of annual giving programs were: (1) Length of time an institution had conducted its program, and (2) amount of money spent.

"Obviously, time alone does not improve alumni fund-raising. It is the *activity* that time allows which generates growth. Time allows an institution to evaluate its needs, develop a plan, prepare a case and organize a program. Time provides an opportunity for the never-ending process of application, evaluation and change to produce improvements. Time makes it possible for well-conceived ideas to become established traditions.

"Likewise, cost (which in my study was the operating expense of an alumni fund) represents all of the materials and services purchased by an institution to conduct a program. Cost reflects a combination of the decisions of the person or persons responsible for conducting the fund. It represents in dollars and cents the attitude of the administrators of an institution toward their fund-raising program.

"The absence of a third factor in the correlation, type of institution, was also significant. In years past, public institutions generally conceded that private schools had greater justification to call upon their alumni for financial support and therefore were more successful than the public schools. The results of my survey indicated that this hypothesis is a myth, and that the success of private institutions was due to the length of time they had spent developing their programs, to the amount of money they had been willing to spend and to other factors related to the operation of their programs or institution, and *not* due to elements associated with them because they were 'private' rather than 'public.'

"The basic fundamental I learned was that the immutable Law of the Harvest has application in fund-raising as well as in growing grain: *As one sows, so shall he reap.*"

—RONALD G. HYDE
Past President
American Alumni Council
Director of Annual Giving
Brigham Young University
Provo, Utah

* * *

"The best advice to a new fund-raiser preparing a campaign plan is: Think like the prospects.

"Prospects have tough questions on their minds. Most of them won't take the trouble to ask these questions; it's your responsibility to anticipate them and provide the answers.

"Prospects want assurance that the people and organization sponsoring the appeal can accomplish the objective for which they are raising money. They want facts which create a credible basis for support of the cause or appeal. Hopes, wishes and ideals must be linked to rational, achievable and necessary objectives.

"Prospects want to be perceived as *people,* not as cards, lists or a mass. People *do* give to people—provided they make the right request. Prospects want to hear 'you' more than 'need.'

"There should be pride in giving, so prospects lean to dignified appeals and eschew mere beggary, sensationalism or emotionalism.

"Most prospects want to join their gift with others to make giving effective; they need assurance their gift is sought in a spirit of universalism among all who should be asked. No one wants to end up as a lone donor.

"If you are satisfied with the answers you give to yourself, the campaign is probably off to a good start."

—STEPHEN WERTHEIMER
Senior Vice President
Oram International Corporation
New York City

* * *

"It's probably more difficult for a veteran to give a few concise words of advice than for a less-seasoned fund-raiser. In one sense, everything is of utmost importance; in another, delightful surprises can occur, but don't count on it.

"A good cause with which the community is familiar and that has a reputation for valuable contributions to health and welfare, or to the common good, or to education and religion, or to the arts has a built-in advantage. But the complete preparation of a time plan with operational strategy and the enlistment of effective volunteer leadership before actually launching a campaign are basic to success.

"Every campaign has its own strong points and its own constituency within the population. These have to be identified. These have to be pursued and emphasized, though your style may vary according to the 'cause,' and enthusiastic tenacity will serve you well in all campaigns and development programs. Never forget the importance of planning and the remarkable accomplishments of dedicated individuals. As every fund-raiser knows, success depends primarily on the planning one does in advance of a campaign."

—ALFRED G. WARDLEY
Fund-raising Consultant
San Francisco, California

* * *

"Assuming you have established your needs carefully and have a solid case on which to base your appeals, I think no aspect of fund-raising is more important than establishing the right atmosphere—in terms of your communications, your volunteer workers and, importantly, your staff (including yourself). You have to be *positive*, optimistic and gently aggressive at all times to keep the entire effort from stalling or simply falling flat.

"Fund-raising is clearly a challenge, but that's the fun of it and, in addition to believing in their cause, the reason why most people keep at it. Your particular constituencies will determine how you best define 'fun,' but I think it is wise to avoid any negativeness or uncertainty if you can. Everyone gains if the undertaking is pleasurable and not looked upon as a chore. If you can build strong momentum through a proper attitude, you should succeed."

—ARTHUR J. HORTON
Recording Secretary
Office of Development
Princeton University
Princeton, New Jersey

* * *

"Essential to success in fund-raising management are elements common to success in living. These elements include integrity, character, enthusiasm, judgment, knowledge, resourcefulness and persistence. Perhaps persistent integrity would be the perfect mix of them all. Nothing in all of the world can take the place of trying again and again. This presupposes integrity—institutional honesty, factual need and case; individual integrity—doing what you can, and honestly following through on every promise of service and support. Without integrity it is pointless to keep on trying. Constant self-examination of program will keep the institution honest, if self-study is done to improve the quality of the service to the served publics. Constant self-improvement of one's skills in communication, logic, motivation and purpose—if done to be a better professional tomorrow than one is today—will do more ultimately to serve an institution, and the giving public as well, than a thousand finely turned phrases in a case statement.

"Remembering Albert Pine's admonition that what we do for ourselves dies with us, and that only what we do for others will remain and become immortal, I would want every fund-raising manager to be selfless in his service. I would like all of us in this profession to feel that we belong to something bigger than ourselves; that we can and do work with others to achieve worthy goals which alone could not be achieved; that we each do our own part, cheerfully; that we know the pride felt in a job well done, and take our moment of glory in humility when (and if) it ever comes; that we are willing to work hard to make our ideas take shape, and that we are in fact helping to build things of lasting value.

"When Huey Long lay dying from an assassin's bullet in September 1935, his final words were, 'God, don't let me die. I have so much to do.' So do I; so do you. Given the opportunities of the fund-raising manager today and into the future, we ought to be able to say we have done our best to make our world a more fit place for another to enjoy."

—BYRON WELCH
President, Welch Associates, Inc.
Houston, Texas

* * *

"Americans are generous people—they want to give to charities. And they will continue to contribute as long as fund-raisers don't abuse their faith. A fund-raiser has to build trust—donors must feel confident that when a fund-raiser promises that their dollars will help needy children or build a theater, these things will happen. Nothing alienates donors more quickly than the feeling they've been duped or misled by a fund-raiser. And then some donors are just naturally wary of fund-raisers, suspecting them of making too large a profit.

"To counter this mistrust and to build faith, a fund-raiser must be credible and accountable. This means full disclosure and informing donors of the results of your campaigns. Let them know what happens to their donations. Be open about your finances. Account for their dollars, even those that pay for fund-raising and administration. In short, accountability creates credibility which means greater fund-raising success."

—HELEN L. O'ROURKE
Vice President
Council of Better Business Bureaus
Director, Philanthropic Advisory Service
Washington, D.C.

* * *

"The first step in fund-raising is to determine your need. In so doing, you must be very clear about your program and purposes. Lack of clarity, confusion, trying to accomplish too much or too little—these are all dangers to avoid. In thinking rationally about needs, you may start from an emotional base. (For example, 'These people are starving and that makes me feel so bad so I want to help them and get others to do so, too'; or 'This facility is crucial for our treatment program and without it we will not be able to meet the needs of many people, let's get the facility built and soon!') Starting from a sense of urgent need yourself, you must then think rationally about how to communicate that need to others so that they will share your feelings and sense of urgency, and contribute to your proposed solution (new building, feeding program, etc.).

"Having carefully identified your needs, you proceed to consider *all* possible sources of funding: individuals, community groups and organizations, foundations, government agencies, corporations and small businesses, etc. Brainstorm, make lists, think boldly and creatively, don't prejudge, assume that everyone is (at least potentially) on your side, for your cause, concerned about your needs and objectives.

"Next, you need to test your prospective funding sources. This is where efficiency and careful monitoring of use of resources are crucial. If you can afford it, seek professional advice from a fund-raising consultant. If you cannot afford professional help, start small and work your way up. Write letters to foundations and tell them what you want to do. Ask for their reports and guidelines so that you know what *they* are looking for in worthwhile projects. Contact members of your board of trustees or advisory council; ask them for leads among corporations, foundations and small businesses. Send appeal letters to selected lists of people who may be sympathetic to your cause. Ask past contributors to increase their gifts in the present.

"Obviously, professional advice can save you money if you are ineffective in your fund-raising efforts. On the other hand, skilled administrators and laypersons with good ideas have often been quite successful on their own. Each situation is unique to some extent; each must be appraised on its own merits.

"Finally, once the fund-raising program is established and going, all of the above elements are endlessly repeated. Continue to determine needs and make them attractive to potential givers. Design fund-raising programs that bring in the most dollars for the least cost. These are the basics of successful fund-raising."

—NEAL H. HURWITZ
Fund-Raising and Promotion Consultant
New York City

* * *

"Volunteers have contributed importantly to the success of American philanthropy. No one can really argue with that. They have walked, washed, called, baked, danced, pleaded, raced and performed in countless other ways in from-the-heart efforts to raise funds for everything from Little League uniforms to music halls and higher education. Nevertheless, you should recognize that unless you choose your volunteers carefully and keep them to the minimum number needed, you may well end up serving them rather than having them serve your cause. Some volunteers will consume a great deal of your time, energy and patience. Some will expect certain material dividends. Some will have their feelings hurt and turn on you and your cause.

"Moral: Be selective about choosing and using volunteers. Look for stability, maturity and a good sense of responsibility. Recruit from your own circle of friends, and then recruit their friends. Have volunteers do only those things that the professional staff cannot do. Make volunteers' work quick, easy and rewarding, and they will stay with you. If you take these precautions, you will be on your way to establishing a strong, productive fund-raising organization from the ground up."

> —DONALD T. NELSON
> Director, The Development Office
> The Church of Jesus Christ
> of Latter-Day Saints
> Provo, Utah

* * *

"When you are writing to ask someone for money, write simply, modestly, honestly. Be specific about what you want. Be cheerful. Write a warm letter—let your humaneness show. Care. Give your reader an opportunity to care, too. Everyone wants to think well of himself—offer the reader an opportunity to strengthen his self-image as someone willing to help others. Ask for specific amounts. Suggest a range of gifts if you are writing to people of different economic levels. Do not say more than you have to say to complete your argument. Do not say less, either—assume the reader knows little about your institution.

"Write to an individual, not to a crowd. Take your time when you are writing. If you don't like to write, find someone who does. Revise your letter until it is as good as you can make it. Then show your letter to people whose intelligence you respect. Listen to them. Rest the material for a day or two. Then revise it to eliminate any major flaws you find, and to make it more persuasive, simpler and quicker to read. Be sure you mail a return vehicle that will identify the donor properly—a card or reply envelope that is either pre-addressed or has spaces for name, address, etc. And do not stop with a single mailing. Send at least one follow-up. If you do not, you will assuredly miss some income that would have reached you. Finally, be sure to thank the donor."

> —CON SQUIRES
> President
> CS Writing and Design Services
> Auburndale, Maine

* * *

"The two most important things a fund-raiser should have before he makes an appointment to ask for a gift are: (1) Thorough knowledge of the institution he is representing and the specific project for which funds are being sought, and (2) as much information as possible about the prospect.

"These both appear to be ridiculously basic, but all of us have been guilty at one time or other of not being prepared. Lack of preparedness invariably leads to substandard gifts or no gifts at all!

"Regardless of how prepared we think we are, it is inevitable that some prospect will ask a question for which we have no answer. I have found that when this occurs, it is usually best to say, 'I do not know, but I will get the answer for you right away.'

"What is the mission of your institution? What are its long-range goals? How does your institution plan to fulfill its mission and accomplish its goals?

"What is your prospect's history of giving to your organization? To other organizations? Where do his interests lie? What is his giving potential?

"If the answers to these questions match your institution and project, your chances for success are bright."

—DWIGHT V. ROBERTS
President
University of Colorado Foundation
Boulder, Colorado

* * *

"Your first responsibility in fund-raising is to develop the needs of your institution and explain them in a convincing manner to your constituency. To explain these needs, you should develop what is called the 'case statement.' This statement must be clear and persuasive in outlining the needs and objectives of your program. Donors are becoming more sophisticated and want to be assured that an institution's needs are urgent and well conceived.

"Your next important step in a major solicitation is to bring the right persons together; that is, to have the right solicitor contact the prospective donor. This was brought home to me in a solicitation for our capital campaign in which we thought for two months about who should call on a certain prospect. After making a suggestion, our president and one of our key trustees made the call. The prospect made the requested commitment immediately and indicated that he knew the president had to be there, but that he was particularly pleased that the trustee had flown 500 miles to make the call. As this case illustrates, the need was made clear, the right persons made the call and the donor responded."

—ROBERT M. HOLCOMBE
Director of Development
Lehigh University
Bethlehem, Pennsylvania

* * *

"I would like to offer six recommendations for successful fund-raising.

"First, choose a realistic goal.

"Second, emphasize special prospects—75 percent of most capital funds and annual giving donations are contributed by 25 percent of the prospects.

"Third, consider a total fund-raising program if your organization is in need of annual as well as capital gifts. A total program should include opportunities for annual and deferred gifts; long-range cultivation of foundations, corporations and large and small businesses; special prospect solicitations and a memorial program.

"Fourth, select a top-flight chairman who is accustomed to dealing with the power structure in your area and support him with the best community leadership available. Divide the group into units headed by division chairmen, and choose wisely people to assist these chairmen. Organization is a key factor in fund-raising.

"Fifth, have related projects available for those who may not be interested in your mainline project. This often creates interest in other aspects of your program.

"Sixth, think positively. Good fund-raising is like the parable of the sower—sow some seeds discriminately, others indiscriminately, because you can never tell which ones will take root."

—ALLEN C. BEST
Former National Director
Community Relations and Development
Literacy Volunteers of America
Syracuse, New York

Chapter Ten

PROFESSIONAL STANDARDS AND GOVERNMENT REGULATIONS

Philanthropic fund-raising, like public office, is a public trust. Fund-raisers depend upon the public for their support, and—if their charities are properly managed—they use that support in the public interest. In a very real sense, then, such fund-raisers are brokers for the public welfare. Consequently, it is right and reasonable that they be accountable to their publics and to the local, state and federal governments under whose aegis they operate.

This chapter introduces you to professional standards and government regulations affecting fund-raising. The intent is not merely to make you aware of the spirit, and—in some cases—the letter of the law, but also to make you a better fund-raiser. Compliance with standards and with intelligently legislated regulation will, inevitably, enhance public confidence and participation in the philanthropic process.

STANDARDS

Over the years, several organizations have promoted constructive standards of fund-raising conduct. Two stand out:

National Information Bureau, Inc. (NIB), and Council of Better Business Bureaus, Inc. (CBBB). In addition, the Commission on Private Philanthropy and Public Needs made some important recommendations in its 1975 report, *Giving in America: Toward a Stronger Voluntary Sector.*

The sections that follow present the standards promulgated by the NIB and CBBB. Because they are practical, positive, sensitive to the needs of both givers and receivers and—in many cases—consistent with existing and pending governmental regulation, you should learn them and make them a part of your way of doing philanthropic business.

National Information Bureau, Inc.

The NIB, established in 1918, is a "not-for-profit, independent watchdog organization" with a twofold purpose: (1) Maintaining sound philanthropic standards, and (2) facilitating wise giving by issuing advisory reports to contributors. When appropriate, the NIB has publicly challenged the practices of certain charities—even the giants—and exposed abuses. The organization issues a monthly bulletin, *Wise Giving Guide,* in which it evaluates hundreds of national charities against eight NIB standards. Fair-minded fund-raisers will find these standards, which are, of course, subject to revision, to be functional and deserving of their support. The standards are printed below with the permission of the NIB.*

NIB Basic Standards in Philanthropy

Philanthropic organizations have a high degree of responsibility because of the public trusteeship involved. Compliance with the following standards, with reasonable evidence supplied on request, is considered essential for approval by the NIB:

---

* Late in 1977 the NIB revised their standards to provide considerably more detail and to clarify their meaning. The reader should contact the NIB for the latest information.

1. *Board*—An active and responsible governing body, serving without compensation, holding regular meetings and with effective administrative control.
2. *Purpose*—A legitimate purpose with no avoidable duplication of the work of other sound organizations.
3. *Program*—Reasonable management efficiency with adequate material and personnel resources to carry on its stated program together with reasonable administration and fund-raising expense.
4. *Cooperation*—Consultation and cooperation with established agencies in the same and related fields.
5. *Ethical Promotion*—Ethical methods of publicity, promotion and solicitation of funds.
6. *Fund-Raising Practice*—
    (a) No payment of commissions for fund-raising.
    (b) No mailing of unordered tickets or merchandise with a request for money in return.
    (c) No general telephone solicitation of the public.
    (d) No use of identified government employees in solicitation of the public.
7. *Audit*—Annual audit employing the Uniform Accounting Standards and prepared by an independent certified public accountant, showing all Support-Revenue and Expenses in reasonable detail. A combined audit of national and affiliates is required. New organizations should provide an independent certified public accountant's statement that a proper financial system has been installed.
8. *Budget*—Detailed annual budget, consistent with the Uniform Accounting Standards employed in the audit report, translating program plans into financial terms.

Council of Better Business Bureaus, Inc.

In August of 1974 the Council of Better Business Bureaus, Inc., published an important, perhaps even a landmark document: *Standards for Charitable Solicitations*. These standards were prepared under the direction of the Philanthropic Advisory Service, a division of the CBBB established to promote ethical standards and public accountability among nonprofit organizations. The document embodied the thinking of hundreds of communicators, charity officers, professional fund-raisers, accountants, direct mail specialists, government officials and advisers from a cross-section of American life.

Unquestionably, the standards this document set forth were the most comprehensive and detailed ever offered to American charities and their publics. They were developed to facilitate, not to frustrate, legitimate fund-raising activities. Specifically, they had two objectives: (1) To serve as a basis for all BBB reports on soliciting organizations, and (2) to provide guidelines for more effective and efficient fund-raising for anyone who was interested.

In July of 1977, the CBBB published expanded and strengthened standards under the same title as those issued originally. These standards—as did the original ones—point the way to more meaningful, rewarding and fulfilling fund-raising for those who ask and for those who give. If you tend to think pretty much in practical terms, be reassured: Compliance is virtually certain to contribute to your fund-raising success.

Specifically, the CBBB standards spell out do's and don'ts concerning the purposes, policy-making and structure, finances, methodology and advertising/informational materials of charitable organizations. They are reprinted in Appendix D.

Like the NIB, the CBBB also publishes a report, *Give But Give Wisely*, issued quarterly, in which it lists charitable, educational and religious organizations that do and do not meet its standards. Number not in compliance as of April 15, 1977: 147!

REGULATION

Federal

For many years the most far-reaching federal law regulating fund-raising activities was the Tax Reform Act of 1969.

It not only altered the tax consequences of charitable giving, but also had major impact on American foundations.

By the mid-1970's, however, pressure was mounting for the enactment of broad-swath federal legislation that would cover all charities. Purpose: to improve public accountability and curb abuses. By the spring of 1977, several bills had been introduced in Congress. The provisions of each differed, but in general their intent was to force charities to: (1) Disclose how much of the money they receive goes to expenses and channel a certain percentage to their exempt charitable purposes, (2) issue annual financial reports. One bill proposed that all charitable organizations—including churches—be subject to the stringent rules that govern private foundations. Another bill took aim at charities that solicit contributions by mail. It was to be administered by the Postal Service and carried a formidable penalty for violators: stoppage of all mail service!

While the final shape of federal legislation is not known at this time, most observers agree that some kind of federal law regulating fund-raising is inevitable—and probably desirable. Ideally, such a law would:

○ Provide for full disclosure, so that charities will, in fact, be accountable to the public. A requirement to report only fund-raising costs is not sufficient. If the public is to evaluate the work of a given charity, it must have information about many aspects of its operation.
○ Protect the interests of the public as well as charities.
○ Avoid overkill. In trying to catch a crook, we sometimes endanger the well-being and effectiveness of law-abiding citizens.
○ Have nationwide applicability, so that if you are in compliance in one state, you are in compliance in all states. Otherwise, individual state registration and compliance requirements will inflict severe administrative and economic hardships on charitable organizatons.

State

By mid-1977, 31 states had passed laws regulating charitable solicitation, and legislation was pending in nine others. This legislation had two origins: (1) The sensational, widely publicized disclosures of fund-raising abuses by certain "charities" in 1975 and 1976, and (2) the cumulative weight of abuses—sensational and otherwise—that had been piling up for many years.

You must, of course, make every effort to comply with state solicitation statutes. Understand, however, that it may not be easy. The difficulty is not with the statutes proper—they are not that demanding—but with two disturbing circumstances:

(1) Most states lack the staff necessary to properly interpret and enforce their statutes. This not only gives dishonest fund-raisers an advantage, it also makes it difficult for you to get answers to questions you may have about a given statute or to receive other kinds of compliance help from the state agency involved.

(2) State statutes vary widely and sometimes wildly in their requirements. This means, for example, that if you are a college fund-raiser appealing by direct mail to alumni in as few as seven or eight states, you may be in compliance in some and breaking the law in others.

It is possible, however, to make some summary-type statements about the various statutes that will help you to understand what is involved and to take the first steps toward compliance. They are as follows:

○ The regulatory agency with which you must deal is usually the office of the secretary of state or attorney general. In Connecticut, Kentucky, New Jersey and Virginia, it is the consumer affairs department.

○ Some states require registration; others, licensing. In some of the states that require licensing, you must prove that you can meet certain standards, such as those contained in *Standards of Accounting and Financial Reporting for Voluntary Health and Welfare Organizations* (available from the National Health Council, 1740 Broadway, New York, N.Y. 10019). Most of the states say that if you raise under a given amount annually—ranging from $250 in Oregon to $10,000 in New York—you need not register or be licensed.

○ Over half of the states have specific cost limitation requirements. In Florida, for example, you can spend up to 25 percent on fund-raising costs and up to another 25 percent for a professional solicitor. Maine has a flat 30 percent ceiling. Minnesota allows you to pay a professional fund-raiser up to 30 percent and New York permits up to 50 percent for mail solicitation using unordered merchandise.

○ Almost all of the states require you to file a financial report. Typically, it is due 60 to 90 days after the close of the fiscal year.

For additional information about state statutes, contact the National Health Council at the address listed above. Your local Better Business Bureau can also help.

City

Many cities, especially the larger ones, have laws regulating charitable solicitation. Begin with the city licensing department and go from there.

Chapter Eleven

WHERE TO GET MORE HELP

There will be moments in fund-raising when you will feel that you are battling the world alone. Frustrations will pile up: Your most faithful volunteer will fall through; someone who ought to know better will sell you short; credit that is rightfully yours will go to another. It happens. Like snakes in the Everglades, it goes with the territory.

When those moments come, permit yourself 15 minutes for self-pity, then straighten your tie—or scarf—and face up to this fact: You are *not* alone. From generations of American fund-raising experience there have evolved hundreds of resources of proven effectiveness that are as close as your telephone, city library or mail box.

Some of the most important of these resources are listed below alphabetically. If you pursue them, you will find answers to questions and needs not provided by this handbook. In addition, these resources will lead you to still others that will deepen your knowledge and extend your effectiveness.

ASSOCIATIONS

American Association of Fund-Raising Counsel, Inc. (AAFC), 500 Fifth Avenue, New York, N.Y. 10036. Although this is an organization of *professional* fund-raising consultants, one of its functions is to serve as a philanthropic information center for "state and federal legislatures, nonprofit institutions and agencies, and students, and others engaged in studies of philanthropy, as well as . . . the general public." Publishes a bulletin 11 times a year, and *Giving USA,* a comprehensive, authoritative annual report of American philanthropy.

Council for the Advancement and Support of Education (CASE), One Dupont Circle, N.W., Suite 600, Washington, D.C. 20036. Serves education through programs in six functional areas: alumni administration, educational fund-raising, government relations, institutional relations/information services, periodicals/publications and executive management. Issues an annual directory, and publishes *CASE Currents,* a nicely edited monthly magazine that always contains at least one technique-oriented article about fund-raising (sample titles: "Writing to Motivate the Heart and the Head" and "What's in It for Me?—How Applied Marketing Can Help Motivate Donors").

Council for Financial Aid to Education, Inc. (CFAE), 680 Fifth Avenue, New York, N.Y. 10019. Created to stimulate ongoing voluntary financial support from as many sources as possible for all U.S. institutions of higher learning. Endeavors to make leaders in business, industry, labor, and civic organizations—as well as the general public—aware of their responsibility to assist higher education financially. Maintains a library and publishes leaflets, survey reports, and staff studies.

Direct Mail Fundraisers Association, Inc. (DMFA), 810 Seventh Avenue, New York, N.Y. 10019. Established to promote direct mail as a fund-raising technique. Also encourages exchange of ideas among members and spells out ethical practices. Issues a quarterly newsletter.

Foundation Center, 888 Seventh Avenue, New York, N.Y.

10019. An educational organization (not an association) established to gather, organize and distribute information about foundations and their grant-making. Maintains a large library (3,700 books, pamphlets, and articles, and 800 bound volumes of annual reports). Issues the *Foundation News* (with its Foundation Grants Index) every other month. Also publishes *The Foundation Directory* and *Foundation Center Source Book*.

The Grantsmanship Center, 1015 West Olympic Blvd., Los Angeles, California 90015. Established to meet "the critical need of nonprofit and public agencies for low-cost training in program planning and resource development." Conducts workshops, maintains a research staff, and publishes *The Grantsmanship Center News*.

National Association for Hospital Development (NAHD), Box 829, Topeka, Kansas 66601. Part of this organization's program is to advance the interests of hospital fund-raising and to promote a better understanding of hospital needs. Issues a quarterly newsletter, semiannual directory and semiannual journal.

National Catholic Development Conference (NCDC), 119 N. Park Avenue, Rockville Centre, New York 11570. Assists its members in finding better ways to raise money. Offers extensive "how to" information. Issues two publications 10 times a year: *Dimensions* and *Fund Raising Forum.* Recently published a comprehensive listing of fund-raising literature, *Bibliography of Fund Raising and Philanthropy.*

National Council on Philanthropy (NCOP), 680 Fifth Avenue, New York, N.Y. 10019. Founded "for the cooperative study of contribution problems, policies and procedures." Authorities at national and regional meetings discuss a range of United States philanthropic concerns, including tax incentives, crime and social justice, support of minority and ecological causes, church fund-raising, etc. Issues *A Voice for Philanthropy* every other month.

National Society of Fund Raisers (NSFR), 1511 K Street, N.W., Suite 831, Washington, D.C. 20005. Promotes fund-raising research and instruction at established learning centers and in other ways. Issues a newsletter eleven times a year and holds workshops and seminars treating all aspects of fund-raising.

PUBLICATIONS

Corporate Giving

Barnes, Norman Kurt. "Rethinking Corporate Charity," *Fortune*, October 1974.

Council for the Advancement and Support of Education. *Matching Gift Details*. Washington, D.C.: Council for Advancement and Support of Education, 1974.

Council for Financial Aid to Education, Inc. *CFAE Casebook: Aid-to-Education Programs of Leading Business Concerns and Guidelines for Corporate Support of Higher Education*. Ninth edition. New York: Council for Financial Aid to Education, 1974.

Eells, Richard. *The Corporation and the Arts*. New York: Interbook, Inc., 1967.

Fremont-Smith, Marion R. *Philanthropy and the Business Corporation*. New York: Russell Sage Foundation, 1972.

McClanahan, Kerry P. "Match Those Gifts!," *CASE Currents*, November 1976.

Foundation Giving

Andrews, F. Emerson. *Foundation Watcher*. Lancaster, Pennsylvania: Franklin and Marshall College, 1973.

Annual Register of Grant Support 1976-1977. Tenth edition. Chicago: Marquis Academic Media, 1976.

Conrad, Daniel L. *The Grants Planner*. San Francisco: The Institute for Fund Raising, 1977.

Cuninggim, Merrimon. *Private Money and Public Service: The Role of Foundations in American Society*. New York: McGraw-Hill Book Company, 1972.

Dermer, Joseph. *The New How to Raise Funds from Foundations*. New York: Public Service Materials Center, 1975.

Dermer, Joseph (editor). *Where America's Large Founda-*

tions Make Their Grants—1977-78 Edition. New York: Public Service Materials Center, 1977.

Directory of the Major American Foundations Supporting Education. Westwood, Massachusetts: J. F. Gray Company, 1975.

The Foundation Center Source Book. 1975-76. Volumes I and II. Irvington-on-Hudson, New York: Columbia University Press, 1975 (Volume I), 1976 (Volume II).

Fund Raising Institute. *Foundation Handbook.* Plymouth Meeting, Pennsylvania: Fund Raising Institute, 1975.

Golden, Hal. *The Grant Seekers: The Foundation Fund Raising Manual.* Dobbs Ferry, New York: Oceana Publications, 1976.

Hillman, Howard, and Abarbanel, Karin. *The Art of Winning Foundation Grants.* New York: Vanguard Press, 1975.

Lewis, Marianna O. (editor). *The Foundation Directory.* Sixth edition. New York: The Foundation Center, 1977.

Margolin, Judith B. *About Foundations.* New edition. New York: The Foundation Center, 1977.

Whitaker, Ben. *The Philanthropoids: Foundations and Society.* New York: William Morrow & Co., Inc., 1974.

White, Virginia P. *Grants . . . How to Find Out About Them and What to Do Next.* New York: Plenum Press, 1975.

PERIODICALS

Bulletin on Public Relations and Development for Colleges and Universities. Gonser Gerber Tinker Stuhr, Public Relations and Development Consultants, 105 West Madison, Chicago, Illinois 60602. Monthly. Distributed without charge to board chairmen, presidents and chief development officers. Offers timely, practical guidelines for college and university fund-raisers. Representative articles: "Achieving Professionalism In Development" and "The Effort To Obtain Major Gifts Should Have Top Priority in a Development Program."

Direct Marketing. Hoke Communications, Inc., 224 Seventh St., Garden City, N.Y. 11530. Monthly. Principal emphasis is on selling merchandise through the mail. However, some of the commercial approaches presented should give you ideas for nonprofit mail solicitation. In addition, each issue gives excellent suggestions for upgrading your solicitation letters.

Foundation News. Council on Foundations, Inc., 888 Seventh Avenue, New York, N.Y. 10019. Every other month. Designed to encourage "a full range of commentary. . ., to increase public understanding of the role of philanthropy, and provide a lively forum for the exchange of information. . . ." Unquestionably, an important publication for anyone seriously interested in obtaining foundation grants. For additional information about *Foundation News,* see the "Foundations" section of Chapter 5.

FRI Newsletter. The Fund Raising Institute, Box 365, Ambler, Pennsylvania 19002. Part of the *FRI Monthly Portfolio.* Consistently contains meaty, down-to-earth ideas to help make you a better fund-raiser. A typical issue is a mix of "how to," case history and items of general interest. Representative articles: "Corporate Support—Is It Worth the Effort?" and "Capital Prospect Leads: Your Local Library May Offer Them."

Fund Raising Management. Hoke Communications, Inc., 224 Seventh St., Garden City, N.Y. 11530. Every other month. A helpful, practical journal that focuses on fund-raising issues, techniques and case histories. Representative feature articles: "Is Your Non-Profit Mail An Invasion of Privacy?" and "How to Use Your Development Committee for Greatest Gain." Department offerings are also useful and include "What's New," "Fund Raising Directory," and "Fund Raiser's Tax Guide."

The Grantsmanship Center News. Grantsmanship Center, 1015 West Olympic Blvd., Los Angeles, California 90015. Six times a year. A well-edited, graphically exciting "how to" journal of fund-raising especially well suited for the nonprofessional. Emphasis is on foundation and governmental grants. Representative feature articles: "How Foundations Review Proposals and Make Grants," "How to Develop A Fund-Raising Strategy," and "Ten Steps To A Million Dollar Fund Raiser."

News Monitor of Philanthropy. Taft Products, Inc., 1000 Vermont Avenue, N.W., Washington, D.C. 20005. Monthly.

Gives a good overview of national philanthropic events, including listings of gifts, bequests and foundation grants. Also reviews books and spotlights accomplished individuals who are in some way associated with fund-raising. The *Monitor* is an informational, not an instructional, publication.

REGULATIONS

National Health Council, Inc. *Viewpoints: State Legislation Regulating Solicitation of Funds from the Public.* 1976 revised edition. New York: National Health Council, Inc., 1976.

TAX-PLANNED GIVING PUBLICATIONS

Several books are available on tax-planned giving, estate planning and related subjects. They are not listed here, however, because they do not reflect changes made by the Tax Reform Act of 1976. Because of the problem of timeliness and currency—one which may grow in severity as pressure mounts for new tax reforms—you would do well to rely on periodicals and related publications for information about tax-planned giving and associated subjects.

Give and Take. Robert F. Sharpe and Company, Inc., 5050 Poplar Avenue/Suite 1222, Memphis, Tennessee 38157. Monthly. "A publication of news and ideas for financial development officers of nonprofit institutions and organizations." No charge for a first subscription addressed to a nonprofit organization. Although one of the principal purposes of *Give and Take* is to promote seminars, cassettes, filmstrips and publications produced by Robert F. Sharpe and Company, it does contain helpful case histories and news items.

J. K. Lasser's Taxes for Fundraisers. J. K. Lasser Tax Institute, Larchmont, New York 10538. Monthly. Describes itself as a "tax report of special interest to development officers and fundraisers of religious and educational institutions, hospitals, and other philanthropic organizations." Cumulatively indexed annually. Subject matter is

technical. Representative articles: "Possible Changes
in the Charitable Contribution Deduction?" and "Can Min-
isters Working For Nonreligious Organizations Claim the
Parsonage Allowance?"

Taxes and Estates. Chemical Bank, Personal Trust Department, 277 Park Avenue, New York, N.Y. 10017. Monthly.
Provides facts and practical illustrations on estate and tax
problems. Subject matter is technical. Representative articles: "What Property Is Subject to the Carryover Basis
Rule?" and "Planning for the Retention of a Business Interest."

Taxwise Giving. Taxwise Giving, 13 Arcadia Road, Old
Greenwich, Connecticut 06870. Monthly. Offers authoritative, current information about tax laws and their impact on
philanthropic giving. Subject matter is technical. Representative articles: "Are Pooled Income Fund Capital Gains
Subject to Minimum Tax?" and "Favorable *Private* Letter
Ruling on Tax-Exempt Charitable Remainder Unitrusts."

In addition to the foregoing tax-planned giving publications, you may purchase an almost endless variety of publications on specific tax-planned giving and estate planning top-
ics from firms specializing in them. Representative titles
include: *Making Your Will . . . What You Should Know Before
You See Your Lawyer, Charitable Remainder Unitrusts, The
Deferred Payment Gift Annuity, What Difference Does A
Will Make?, How the New Tax Reform Act Affects Your Giving,* and *The State Has Made Your Will!* Unit cost varies, of
course, depending on the size and features of each publication. A typical price for a 24-page brochure is 40¢ . If you order 1,000 or more, for a slight additional charge you can have
your organization's name, address and telephone number imprinted. These publications offer two major advantages: (1)
They almost put tax and estate-planning experts on your staff,
and (2) they provide the very latest information—an important consideration at a time when tax laws are subject to fre-
quent changes. Publishers include: Kennedy-Sinclaire, 524
Hamburg Turnpike, Wayne, New Jersey 07470; Robert F.
Sharpe and Company, Inc., 5050 Poplar Avenue/Suite 1222,
Memphis, Tennessee 38157; and Taxwise Giving, 13 Arcadia
Road, Old Greenwich, Connecticut 06870.

APPENDIX A

FORTY LEADING U.S. PRIVATE FOUNDATIONS RANKED BY PAYMENT OF GRANTS (millions $)

Foundation	1975	1976	Chief Interests
Ford Foundation	162.7	156.8	Public welfare across broad spectrum
Lilly Endowment, Inc.	53.5	51.9	Education, religion, community development
The Rockefeller Foundation	42.9	46.9	Hunger, population, international relations, education in developing countries, equal opportunity, cultural development, environment
The Robert Wood Johnson Foundation	33.3	43.6	Advancement of U. S. health
The Andrew W. Mellon Foundation	34.2	35.7	Education, health, cultural projects, conservation, civic programs
W. K. Kellogg Foundation	23.0	33.0	Education, health, agriculture
The Pew Memorial Trust	28.4	—	Hospitals, medical research, education, church-related institutions, civic, cultural activities.
The Kresge Foundation	27.8	25.6	Building construction and equipment involving higher education, hospitals, conservation, and the arts
The Duke Endowment	20.5	22.7	Physical, mental and spiritual needs of mankind
Carnegie Corp. of New York	14.4	13.6	Higher education, early childhood education and certain aspects of elementary and secondary education
Alfred P. Sloan Foundation	12.4	13.0	Science, technology, education, economics, management
Richard King Mellon Foundation	12.3	12.7	Education, health, civic and cultural development, urban affairs
Charles Stewart Mott Foundation	13.4	11.0	Adult education and recreation

Foundation			
Rockefeller Brothers Fund, Inc.	9.9	10.4	International affairs, economic and social development, equal rights, conservation, religion, education, visual and performing arts
The Edna McConnell Clark Foundation	5.4	8.4	Children, elderly, poor, and people of the developing world
The Vincent Astor Foundation	8.1	8.1	Educational and community service programs for children and older people
Frank E. Gannett Newspaper Foundation, Inc.	6.3	8.1	Health, welfare, and well-being of those in communities served by Gannett businesses
William Penn Foundation	7.9	7.6	Education, culture, health, conservation, social welfare
Houston Endowment, Inc.	9.0	7.2	Higher education
Surdna Foundation, Inc.	5.3	7.1	Higher education, aid to handicapped, medical research
The Bush Foundation	7.3	7.1	Higher education, performing arts and humanities, health care, social/welfare agencies
The Commonwealth Fund	5.2	6.5	Improvement of medical education
Max C. Fleischmann Foundation	5.4	6.4	Educational buildings and equipment, scholarships, and research in medical/biological sciences
The Robert A. Welch Foundation	6.4	6.3	Research, lectureships, professorships, and scholarships in chemistry
The James Irvine Foundation	3.9	5.8	Health, education, youth service
William R. Kenan, Jr., Charitable Trust	4.8	5.2	Endowed professorships bearing the donor's name
The Charles A. Dana Foundation, Inc.	3.5	5.0	Higher education and medical research
Northwest Area Foundation	4.2	4.9	Education, health, physical and social sciences, arts and humanities
Charles Hayden Foundation	2.6	4.6	Physical facilities and equipment for organizations serving youth

FORTY LEADING U.S. PRIVATE FOUNDATIONS RANKED BY PAYMENT OF GRANTS (millions $) – cont.

Foundation	1975	1976	Chief Interests
John Simon Guggenheim Memorial Foundation	4.4	4.6	Improve educational, literary, artistic and scientific power of America and promote international understanding
Charles F. Kettering Foundation	4.2	4.5	Education, science, international affairs, and urban affairs
Amon G. Carter Foundation	2.0	4.5	Higher and secondary education, youth, arts, child welfare, hospitals
Mary Flagler Cary Charitable Trust	5.1	4.5	Conservation of natural resources and music
Z. Smith Reynolds Foundation, Inc.	4.4	4.0	Education, hospitals, public health, libraries, and recreation
The George Gund Foundation	3.0	3.8	Education and help for the disadvantaged
Claude Worthington Benedum Foundation	2.9	3.8	Higher education, health, youth development
Sarah Mellon Scaife Foundation	6.2	3.4	Higher education, urban projects, hospitals and medical education, ecology, fine arts, oceanography, animal welfare
Smith Richardson Foundation, Inc.	3.4	3.3	Creative leadership and historic restoration
Research Corporation	3.2	3.1	Research in natural sciences and in programs to combat nutritional diseases
The John A. Hartford Foundation, Inc.	4.0	3.1	Biomedical research

IMPORTANT NOTE: Many of these foundations restrict grants to their own geographical areas. Consult *The Foundation Directory* for complete information.

SOURCE: American Association of Fund-Raising Counsel, Inc.

APPENDIX B

PARTIAL LISTING OF COMMUNITY FOUNDATIONS BY GEOGRAPHICAL AREA

Foundation Name	Address	Principal Interests
NEW ENGLAND AREA		
Bridgeport Area Foundation, Inc.	955 Main St., Room 508 Bridgeport, Conn. 06603	Wide range of community-oriented projects
Committee of the Permanent Charity Fund	One Boston Place Boston, Mass. 02108	Social services, welfare, health, education
New Hampshire Charitable Fund	One South St. Concord, N.H. 03301	Humanities, education, environment, recreation, health
Rhode Island Foundation	15 Westminister St. Providence, R.I. 02903	Youth, elderly, health, education, arts, culture
MIDDLE ATLANTIC AREA		
Buffalo Foundation	812 Genesee Building Buffalo, N.Y. 14202	Education, social welfare
Central New York Community Foundation	423 West Onondaga St. Syracuse, N.Y. 13202	Social and welfare programs
New York Community Trust	415 Madison Ave. New York, N.Y. 10017	Welfare, education, community development, culture
Philadelphia Foundation	Two Girard Plaza, Suite 1502 Philadelphia, Penn. 19102	Family/social services, health, education, children/youth/elderly

Foundation Name	Address	Principal Interests
Pittsburgh Foundation	301 Fifth Ave., Suite 1417 Pittsburgh, Penn. 15222	Community welfare, children/youth, education, civic, culture, health

GREAT LAKES AREA

Foundation Name	Address	Principal Interests
Aurora Foundation	32 South Water St. Aurora, Ill. 60504	Hospitals, higher education, community service
Chicago Community Trust	208 South LaSalle St. Suite 850 Chicago, Ill. 60604	Health, social service, civic affairs
Cleveland Foundation Resources	700 National City Bank Building Cleveland, Ohio 44114	Education, culture, health/welfare, civic affairs
Columbus Foundation	17 South High St. Suite 707 Columbus, Ohio 43215	Social service, arts/humanities, hospitals/health, education
Grand Rapids Foundation	300 C Waters Building Grand Rapids, Mich. 49502	Social welfare, education, hospitals, arts
Greater Cincinnati Foundation	Gas & Electric Building Cincinnati, Ohio 45202	Education, handicapped, health, arts, social welfare

Indianapolis Foundation	119 English Foundation Building 615 North Alabama St. Indianapolis, Ind. 46204	Welfare, health, elderly, education, civic affairs, culture
Kalamazoo Foundation	332 ISB Building 151 South Rose St. Kalamazoo, Mich. 49007	Community development, youth and elderly, education, culture
Milwaukee Foundation	161 West Wisconsin Ave. Milwaukee, Wis. 53202	Arts, education, community welfare, health
Minneapolis Foundation	400 Foshay Tower 821 Marquette Ave. Minneapolis, Minn. 55402	Social welfare, education, arts, health, religion, conservation
Saint Paul Foundation	355 Washington St. Paul, Minn. 55101	Education, culture, health, welfare

MID-AMERICA AREA

Denver Foundation	70 West Sixth Ave. Suite 310 Denver, Colo. 80204	Social services, education, youth and senior citizens, civic affairs, culture
Lincoln Foundation, Inc.	215 Centennial Mall South Lincoln, Nebr. 68508	Physical, mental and moral progress

SOUTHEAST AREA

Greater Birmingham Foundation	2201 Crest Road Birmingham, Ala. 35209	Health, welfare, youth, culture, education

PARTIAL LISTING OF COMMUNITY FOUNDATIONS BY GEOGRAPHICAL AREA

Foundation Name	Address	Principal Interests
Greater Kanawha Valley Foundation	818 Virginia St. E. Charleston, W. Va. 25301	General welfare
Norfolk Foundation	400 Royster Building Norfolk, Va. 23510	Health, scholarships, culture, community projects
Spartanburg County Foundation	545 Montgomery Building Spartanburg, S.C. 29301	Education, welfare, arts/humanities
Winston-Salem Foundation	2230 Wachovia Building Winston-Salem, N.C. 27101	Education, welfare, health, arts/ humanities

SOUTHWEST AREA

Dallas Community Chest Trust Fund, Inc.	4605 Live Oak St. Dallas, Tex. 75204	Promote human welfare
Oklahoma City Community Foundation, Inc.	1300 North Broadway Oklahoma City, Okla. 73103	Education, culture, hospitals, performing arts, youth

FAR WEST AREA

California Community Foundation	P. O. Box 54303 Terminal Annex Los Angeles, Calif. 90054	Welfare, health, children/youth
Pasadena Foundation	16 North Marengo Ave. Pasadena, Calif. 91101	Child, youth and senior citizen welfare
Riverside Foundation	3900 Market St. Riverside, Calif. 92501	Education, welfare

180

San Francisco Foundation	425 California St. Suite 1602 San Francisco, Calif. 94104	Welfare, health, education, community problems, arts/humanities
Santa Barbara Foundation	11 East Carrillo St. Santa Barbara, Calif. 93101	Community service, culture, scholar-ship loans

PACIFIC NORTHWEST AREA

Seattle Foundation	Joshua Green Building Room 520 Seattle, Wash. 98101	Health, welfare, education, humanities

SOURCES: *Giving USA 1977 Annual Report* and various foundation publications.

APPENDIX C

HIGHER EDUCATIONAL INSTITUTIONS ATTRACTING THE MOST PHILANTHROPIC SUPPORT—
1969 THROUGH 1976 (GIFTS AND BEQUESTS)
(RANKED BY STANDING AS OF 1975–1976) (millions $)

LARGER COLLEGES AND UNIVERSITIES

Institution	1969–70	1970–71	1971–72	1972–73	1973–74	1974–75	1975–76
Harvard University	52.1	60.9	46.5	57.2	56.8	52.4	59.0
Univ. of California	26.0	47.3	35.5	44.3	37.1	40.2	57.5
Stanford University	30.3	29.2	32.7	46.5	41.8	45.1	41.8
Yale University	32.0	45.4	43.4	32.2	44.1	27.4	37.7
Univ. of Penn.	26.1	20.8	21.9	28.9	24.6	34.0	31.7
Columbia University	31.6	35.6	33.1	27.1	30.0	21.4	29.8
Univ. of Minnesota	13.0	14.8	16.3	20.4	26.3	26.4	27.1
Case Western Reserve University	10.6	16.1	15.9	18.2	19.0	18.4	26.6
Univ. of Chicago	38.2	28.2	24.1	28.7	26.3	24.5	26.6
Cornell University	24.3	25.6	27.4	30.6	32.6	26.1	26.2
Univ. of Southern California	13.8	19.1	15.7	18.8	16.4	19.2	26.1
Mass. Institute of Technology	19.6	39.6	22.1	21.7	22.7	20.3	22.4
Princeton University	18.5	21.8	27.2	22.1	19.0	19.2	22.2
Univ. of Illinois	9.8	10.8	10.1	14.2	12.9	14.0	20.6
New York University	37.7	21.7	28.5	26.9	24.6	19.7	19.2
Johns Hopkins University and Hospital	9.7	11.2	12.8	14.4	18.5	15.7	17.9
Dartmouth	21.1	17.4	15.2	16.7	16.4	10.7	16.2

Institution							
Northwestern University	23.5	16.9	14.9	30.3	21.0	16.6	16.1
Ohio State University	6.3	4.4	5.4	10.2	9.5	10.2	9.3
Tulane University	7.5	7.7	7.2	8.4	9.9	10.1	8.9
Notre Dame University	7.7	9.3	7.6	9.2	7.1	7.1	8.1
University of Cincinnati	8.7	10.5	7.7	11.7	5.2	15.6	7.6
Brown University	7.7	5.4	7.5	8.7	7.1	10.6	7.3
Carnegie-Mellon University	4.4	6.6	4.2	6.3	4.7	4.0	7.3
Univ. of Iowa	4.7	4.5	9.6	5.7	5.7	8.8	7.2
Lehigh University	3.4	2.9	3.4	3.7	4.8	6.5	7.0
Loyola University of Chicago	12.6	11.2	13.3	19.1	13.2	6.5	6.7

SMALLER COLLEGES AND UNIVERSITIES

Institution							
Stevens Institute of Technology	1.9	1.1	1.0	1.2	3.0	1.0	8.4
Carleton College	2.6	2.3	2.0	1.9	3.7	4.3	5.1
Williams College	4.3	5.7	4.4	6.1	5.6	5.3	5.0
Antioch College	1.0	1.1	1.1	.7	.9	.6	3.7
Middlebury College	1.3	1.4	1.9	1.9	2.1	2.5	3.1
Bowdoin College	2.3	2.0	1.6	3.6	4.0	4.2	2.9
Haverford College	.8	1.3	2.4	3.3	1.3	2.1	2.4
Trinity College	1.4	1.9	4.0	1.9	1.6	1.9	2.3
Wesleyan University	2.5	1.0	1.0	1.6	3.1	1.1	2.2
Beloit College	1.6	.7	1.5	2.0	1.5	1.4	2.0
Colby College	2.1	2.0	1.6	1.2	1.1	2.7	2.0
Hobart and William Smith Colleges	1.2	.8	1.2	1.0	1.2	1.8	1.8
Bucknell University	3.0	1.2	1.1	1.1	1.0	.8	1.8

SOURCE: Brakeley, John Price Jones Inc.

APPENDIX D
Standards for
Charitable Solicitations
Council of Better Business Bureaus, Inc.*

FOREWORD

Traditionally, Better Business Bureaus, with the cooperation of concerned business organizations, have been responsible for promoting the establishment of standards of ethical conduct in many areas.

To encourage public support of reputable philanthropic endeavors and to advance high standards of ethical conduct among all soliciting organizations, the Better Business Bureaus have developed these basic standards relating to the structure, finances, fund-raising methods, and the advertising and informational materials of such organizations. They are not intended to restrict charitable solicitations but are issued in the belief that both the general public and soliciting organizations will benefit by full and accurate disclosure of all information which potential donors may need and reasonably

*Issued August, 1974; Second Printing May, 1976; Revised 1977.
Copyright © 1974, 1977 Council of Better Business Bureaus, Inc. 1150 17th Street, N.W., Washington, D.C. 20036. Reprinted with permission from the Council of Better Business Bureaus, Inc.

wish to consider in a decision on where their help is needed and how well their contributions of time and money will be utilized.

These standards apply to organizations ruled tax exempt under section 501 (c) (3) of the Internal Revenue Code, other than private foundations, and to all other organizations which conduct charitable solicitations by any means. They do not apply to hospitals, schools and colleges, churches, or fraternal, civic, professional or trade groups conducting an appeal which is

(1) confined and directed exclusively to the organization's voting membership or alumni;

(2) an invitation to voting membership (unless directed to the general public, with a contribution being the only requirement for membership); or

(3) a request for support without any charitable purpose associated with the appeal.

Organizations not covered by the BBB STANDARDS are encouraged to disclose fully all information which members, alumni or contributors might reasonably wish to consider.

Professional and technical assistance in the development of these standards were provided by representatives of media, charitable organizations, the accounting profession, professional fund raisers, fund-raising and direct mail firms, corporate contribution advisors and Better Business Bureaus.

Adherence to these standards by all soliciting organizations will inspire public confidence, further the growth of public participation in philanthropy and advance the objectives of responsible private initiative and self-regulation.

DEFINITIONS

A. "Charitable solicitation" is any oral or written request made directly or indirectly for money, credit, property, financial assistance, volunteer service or other thing of value (to be given now or on a deferred basis) on the plea, representation or implication that it will be used for charitable, patriotic, benevolent, educational, civic, fraternal or other philanthropic purposes. It does not mean an appeal conducted by a hospital, school or college, church, or fraternal, civic, professional or trade group if the appeal (1) is confined and directed exclusively to the organization's voting membership or alumni; (2) is an invitation to voting membership (unless directed to the general public, with a contribution being the only requirement for membership); or (3) is a request for support without any charitable purpose associated with the appeal.

B. "Soliciting organization" is any group, corporation, association, partnership or individual engaged in a charitable solicitation.

C. The "public" includes, but is not limited to, groups, corporations, foundations, institutions and individuals.

D. "Voting membership" is those members of a soliciting organization who participate in the election of the members of the governing board of that organization and approve the actions of the board.

E. "Voting trusteeship" is the membership of the governing board of a soliciting organization either at the national or local level. The voting trusteeship is responsible for the policies, programs and financial management of a soliciting organization.

F. "Advertising and informational material" includes, but is not limited to, advertising, informational and educational material in print and broadcast media, paid and public service announcements, direct mail, window display signs, counter cards, public notices, canisters, brochures and flyers.

PART ONE
PURPOSES, POLICY-MAKING, FINANCES AND FUND-RAISING METHODS

I.   *General Requirements*

A. A soliciting organization shall disclose upon request the ruling of the Internal Revenue Service regarding its tax-exempt status.

B. A soliciting organization shall disclose, upon request, whether or not it is qualified to receive contributions deductible for federal, state and local income tax purposes.

C. A soliciting organization shall disclose, upon request, information about its activities, finances and voting trusteeship, including information and documents necessary to substantiate compliance with these standards.

D. A soliciting organization shall be operated in accordance with its stated purposes and applicable Federal, state and local laws and regulations including those relating to nondiscriminatory practices.

II. *Purposes and Programs*

A. Soliciting organizations shall have a written statement of purpose which shall serve as the basis for and be described in all charitable solicitations.

B. Should eligibility to benefit from an organization's program be limited for any reason (e.g., specific facilities, geographical areas or classes of persons), such limitations shall be clearly and fully disclosed in all charitable solicitaticns.

III. *Policy-Making and Structure*

A. Soliciting organizations shall have an active governing body which meets with reasonable frequency and attendance, and which operates under by-laws ensuring an adequate voting trusteeship. If the governing body meets only once annually, there shall be additional meetings by a committee of board members having interim policy-making authority.

B. Soliciting organizations shall have a responsible governing body which avoids business transactions in which board members, staff, or their family have a financial interest.

C. Compensation of any members of the governing body by soliciting organizations is strongly discouraged; and in any case, compensated members shall never constitute more than twenty percent of those voting in any decision of the governing body or committee to which interim policy-making authority is delegated. "Compensation" as here used includes direct or indirect payment for services rendered in any capacity, but does not include expenses to attend board meetings.

D. Upon request, soliciting organizations shall disclose clearly the responsibilities, organization, and decision-making structure of the governing body, any interim policy-making committees, and advisory committees, including the frequency of and attendance at meetings.

E. Upon request, soliciting organizations shall disclose clearly the function, responsibilities and location of national, regional and local offices and facilities, as well as the relationship with any affiliated organizations.

IV. *Finances*

A. Soliciting organizations shall obtain and make available upon request an annual, externally audited financial statement with the auditor's report and notes.

B. A soliciting organization's annual financial statements shall be prepared in accordance with generally accepted accounting principles and reporting practices, and shall be audited by a qualified independent accountant in accordance with generally accepted auditing standards.

C. The report of the independent auditor on a soliciting organization's annual financial statements shall be without significant qualification.

D. Soliciting organizations shall include in their annual financial report to the public all income and all costs for fund-raising activities including special events.

E. An organization receiving a substantial portion of its public support through entities controlled by or closely affiliated with it shall disclose fully all income and all costs associated with fund-raising activities conducted on its behalf by such entities.

F. Soliciting organizations shall provide upon request a full accounting of gross receipts, total expenses, and income accruing to the organization for whose benefit the charitable solicitation was conducted.

G. Soliciting organizations shall report as fund-raising expenses all direct and indirect costs related to activities and materials that are an integral and inseparable part of any charitable solicitation.

H. Soliciting organizations shall spend a reasonable percentage of total income (from all sources) directly for program services, as distinct from fund raising and management-and-general; and fund raising costs shall not be excessive in relation to total contributions.

V.   *Fund-Raising*

A. Soliciting organizations shall provide to the public at the time of an appeal a clear and concise description of the programs and special projects for which contributions are being solicited.

B. Soliciting organizations shall not pay commissions, kick-backs, finders' fees, percentages, bonuses or over-rides for any fund-raising activity, including telephone, door-to-door, direct mail or other method.

C. Soliciting organizations mailing unordered items (e.g., pens, seals, name labels, ties and stamps) shall clearly disclose that recipients are under no obligation to pay for or return any items received.

D. Any offer for sale of merchandise made in conjunction with a charitable solicitation shall clearly disclose the amount or percentage of money from the sale which will actually go to the organization for whose benefit the appeal is made.

E. Soliciting organizations shall not mail appeals disguised as invoices, bills or statements of account.

F. Any telephone appeal shall accurately disclose at

the outset of the call (1) the name of the soliciting organization, (2) the purpose of the call, (3) whether the organization is for-profit or nonprofit, and (4) how further information can be obtained.

G. A soliciting organization shall provide to all individuals who approach the public for the purpose of charitable solicitation, an identification card or badge containing its name and address and the individual's name. If applicable law requires solicitor identification which is provided by the jurisdiction, such identification shall suffice.

H. Soliciting organizations shall maintain adequate systems of control over contributions, including procedures specified in the Audit Guides published by the American Institute of Certified Public Accountants.

I. Soliciting organizations shall not use techniques of intimidation or harassment, including threats of public disclosure or economic retaliation.

J. Soliciting organizations providing goods, admission to fund-raising activities (such as testimonial dinners and theater parties), or other services in return for payment shall clearly disclose upon request the portion of payment which constitutes a charitable contribution for tax purposes.

K. Soliciting organizations shall not publicize the identity of contributors without obtaining prior written permission.

L. Soliciting organizations shall, upon request, remove a person's name from their mailing list.

M. Soliciting organizations shall not disclose or use the name of any person, organization or company in any oral or written solicitation without obtaining advance written authority to do so.

N. A soliciting organization shall not solicit funds for the benefit of, or in the name of, another organization unless it has written permission from the benefiting organization to do so. The soliciting organization shall provide full financial reports in accordance with section IV.D. of Part One of these standards.

PART TWO
ADVERTISING AND INFORMATIONAL MATERIALS

The following standards shall apply to all advertising and informational materials directed to the contributing public by charitable organizations, in whatever form and by whatever means, including, but not limited to, print and broadcast media, direct mail literature, window display signs, counter cards, public notices, canisters, brochures and flyers. They are intended as guidelines to assure that all public communications accurately and factually represent the purposes, needs, programs and services of charitable organizations.

I. *Basic Principles*

    A. The responsibility for truthful and nondeceptive advertising and informational materials rests with the soliciting organization and the entity which prepares and assembles such materials.

    B. Advertisements and informational materials shall not be untrue, misleading, deceptive or fraudulent in whole or in part.

    C. Advertisements or informational materials may be considered misleading as a whole although every sentence separately considered is literally true. Misrepresentation may result not only from direct statements but by omitting or obscuring material facts.

    D. Soliciting organizations shall be prepared to substantiate any statements or claims made before publication and, upon request, present such substantiation promptly to the advertising medium, the Better Business Bureau and the public.

    E. Any description or reference to a program or service by a soliciting organization shall be factual and accurate.

II. *General Requirements*

    A. Advertising and informational materials shall not disparage any person or group on grounds of sex, race, color, creed, age, nationality, mental or physical condition or social status.

B. Statistical data shall be based on factual or representative situations.

C. Any financial summary included in informational materials shall accurately reflect the overall financial picture as presented in the organization's financial statements.

D. Any claims and promises shall accurately reflect existing conditions, situations and circumstances.

E. An asterisk may be used to impart additional information about a word or term which is not in itself inherently deceptive. An asterisk, footnote or other reference symbol should not be used as a means of contradicting or substantially changing the meaning of any advertising statement.

III. *Disclosure Requirements*

A. Soliciting organizations shall disclose the following in all advertising and informational materials (see exception in B. below):

1. The name of the soliciting organization and the source from which the public may obtain additional information regarding the organization's programs and services.

2. A statement as to whether or not the organization is qualified to receive contributions deductible for federal, state and local income tax purposes.

3. A statement of the purpose for which the soliciting organization was established.

4. A clear statement of any limitations to benefit from the soliciting organization's program.

5. A clear and concise description of programs and special projects for which contributions are being solicited.

6. A clear statement disclosing the amount or percentage of money derived from the sale of merchandise which will actually go to the organization for whose benefit the appeal is made.

B. If, due to time and space limitations in advertising (i.e., spot announcements or small print ads), it is impracticable and economically unfeasible to make any disclosure (except III.A.1. relating to the source for additional information which is required in all cases), the soliciting organization shall in any event file the required disclosures with the medium along with its proposed advertising.

IV. *Layout and Illustrations*

A. The composition and layout of advertising and informational materials shall be such as to minimize the possibility of misunderstanding by the reader.
B. Photographs, films and illustrations of programs, services or recipients of aid shall be accurate and typical representations of the programs, services and recipients of aid of the soliciting organization.
C. If models are used to portray recipients of aid or beneficiaries of programs and services, clear disclosure of that fact shall be made in immediate conjunction with the portrayal.
D. If photographs are used, dates and sources shall be disclosed if failure to do so would be misleading.

V. *Testimonials and Endorsements*

A. Statements in advertising and informational materials by doctors, dentists, nurses or other professional people shall be presented by members of such professions reciting actual experience, or it shall be made apparent from the presentation itself that the portrayal is dramatized. No such presentation may be placed on television except in the context of a public service announcement approved by the broadcast medium.
B. Persons making testimonials, endorsements, or who are pictured in advertising or informational materials shall be identified as to their relationship with

the organization and their actual experience with the organization's programs and services.

C. If an endorser has a direct pecuniary interest in the organization whose program or service is being endorsed, this shall be disclosed in the advertisement or informational materials.

D. Testimonials or endorsements shall be quoted in their entirety, unless failure to do so does not alter the overall meaning and impact of the testimonial or endorsement.

E. Testimonials and endorsements shall be genuine and represent the current opinion of the endorser.

F. If the endorser is associated with some well-known and highly regarded institution, the endorsement shall clearly disclose whether the endorser speaks in a personal capacity or on behalf of such institution.

G. Advertising and informational materials shall not use an endorsement or approval by indefinitely large or vague groups, such as "the doctors of America."

INDEX